ALIVENESS MINDSET

LEAD AND LIVE WITH MORE PASSION, PURPOSE, AND JOY

JACK CRAVEN

Forefront
BOOKS

Published by Forefront Books, Nashville, Tennessee.
Distributed by Simon & Schuster.

Library of Congress Control Number: 2023923590

Print ISBN: 978-1-63763-261-1
E-book ISBN: 978-1-63763-262-8

Cover Design by Faceout Studio
Interior Design by Bill Kersey, KerseyGraphics

Printed in the United States of America

To my wife and partner-in-all things,
Judy. Thanks for changing my life.

My love forever.

CONTENTS

Introduction: Aliveness Starts with You 7

PART I: INTRODUCING ALIVENESS
1: This Is What I Want 15
2: The Circle of Aliveness. 23
3: More Than a Nice Concept 37
4: Show Up or Shut Up. 49

PART II: ALIVENESS MINDSET
5: It's All in Your Head 59
6: Look in the Mirror *Aliveness Mindset 1: Ownership* 69
7: Accessing the Energy Within *Aliveness Mindset 2: Openness*. 79
8: The First Step to (Any) Change *Aliveness Mindset 3: Awareness* 93
9: The Best You Is the Real You *Aliveness Mindset 4: Authenticity* 105
10: Overcoming Fear *Aliveness Mindset 5: Courage*. 119
11: Play the Long Game *Aliveness Mindset 6: Tenacity*. 129
12: Connection Is Everything *Aliveness Mindset 7: Love*. 139

PART III: ALIVENESS PRACTICE
13: Feel It: Your Personal Brand of Aliveness 157
14: Lock It In: Your Anchoring Mindsets. 169
15: Live It: Aligned with Aliveness 183

PART IV: OPTIMAL STATE
16: How Do I Know?. 197
17: Aliveness is The Rule, Not the Exception 205
18: Living All In (LAI) Tools 217
Conclusion: The Future Is Alive 241

Glossary. 245
Acknowledgments 247
About the Author 251
Notes 253

ALIVENESS STARTS WITH YOU

As I was screaming in a conference room at the Chaminade resort in Santa Cruz, surrounded by twenty other business leaders, I realized you don't get to choose your epiphanies. They just happen.

My particular epiphany was simple: *I was angry*. On a deep, subconscious level that I had not admitted to anyone, including myself, I was lonely, unhappy, frustrated, and desperate for change.

I had no idea just how much needed to change. It was April 29, 2012, and I was attending a leadership retreat led by Jim Dethmer and Diana Chapman, cofounders of what would later become the Conscious Leadership Group (CLG). Going into the retreat, I was not planning on doing any screaming. I had every reason to be satisfied and excited about life. I was a happily married husband and the father of three girls. I had a law degree, which had been my dream as a teenager, and I had worked as a trial lawyer for the State's Attorney's Office in Chicago before going into private practice. After practicing law for five years, I decided to pivot and went into my family's business selling closeout consumer products to wholesalers and retail chains across North America. I was CEO of that business for almost twenty years. We experienced tremendous growth, and we adapted and reinvented ourselves to overcome numerous challenges.

On the outside, I was successful and stable. I was an achiever, a visionary, a connector. I was someone people looked to for leadership and execution. I liked that. Checking things off my list gave me a rush. Tackling challenges and solving problems seemed to be what I was built for, and I ran full force at every obstacle I faced.

I was not in a healthy place on the inside. To deal with the inner void, I assumed more and more responsibility, which only deepened my sense of loneliness and frustration. The harder I worked, the worse I felt. I came to the point where I was putting in ten-hour days, six or seven days a week. I would often wake up at three in the morning in a state of anxiety, and I would start working just to stay caught up on everything I had on my plate.

I was living the polar opposite of a healthy, fulfilled existence, but I didn't know anything else. That was my normal.

Even though I was unhappy, I was always surprised when people told me I seemed serious, even somber. I guess I thought that because I didn't admit my frustration to myself, it wasn't visible to anyone else. Those comments were strange to me since I had always been a funny, happy person. Years before, I'd performed multiple times as a stand-up comic and done well. I always had a natural public presence and a quick sense of humor, and people typically liked and trusted me. What was happening?

I knew I should feel content, so I convinced myself I was. In actuality, I was living a life filled with obligations that I blamed on others. I *had* to be a great husband, a great father, a great son, a great brother, and a great CEO. I had to be perfect. I couldn't fail.

People depended on me. I didn't have the luxury of choosing a different path.

Or so I told myself.

That was my mental state when I arrived at the retreat. As a member of a business peer group called Young Presidents' Organization (YPO), I had attended many traditional leadership trainings. Within an hour, though, I realized this wasn't a typical leadership retreat. They didn't even have an agenda. We weren't there to learn from speakers at podiums, they said. We were there to help each other become more "conscious" as leaders. Whatever that meant.

At one point, we went around the room sharing why we were there. When it was my turn, I shared my story and why I chose to attend. I said I felt stuck both professionally and personally. I wanted support on how to reduce my suffering. I wanted to be happier. I wanted...actually, I hardly knew what I wanted. I just knew that it wasn't to keep doing what I was doing.

Jim and Diana asked me if I wanted to let go of any anger. That surprised me. I wasn't angry, I thought. I just wasn't happy. Back then, I didn't even realize I was feeling anger, let alone suppressing it.

They suggested that I scream to release what had built up inside. Normally I'd be concerned about how I looked to a roomful of leaders I had just met, but I had been optionless for so long I was willing to try anything to release my fears and frustrations. I felt angry that my work life wasn't fulfilling, and scared that I felt stuck and didn't know what to do.

I didn't realize how much emotion I was repressing until I started screaming. Again. And again. And *again*. Until my voice was hoarse. When I stopped screaming, I felt raw, vulnerable, and embarrassed. But I also felt lighter. The other leaders that weekend were surprised yet supportive. (And I had no reason to be embarrassed; others faced similar challenges and experienced their own epiphanies. I'll share more about their reactions to mine in chapter 6.)

I knew that I wasn't going to keep pretending anymore. I wasn't going to keep burying my feelings. I didn't know how it was going to happen, but I knew I was determined to make changes.

And I did.

When I look back on that weekend, I can see how many things began to shift that day. It was imperceptible at first, but over time a monumental change occurred. I began to take seriously the questions my heart had been asking all along. What did I want out of life? What was I searching for? And just as importantly, why was I resisting the answers?

I didn't have the words for it then, but I was on a search for aliveness. *My aliveness.* That deep, inner satisfaction that comes from being authentically yourself, fully aligned and engaged and connected.

This book was born out of that time of wrestling with myself, along with my years of leadership coaching since then. Since transitioning to becoming an executive coach in 2015, I've worked with hundreds of business leaders who are on that same search. This book contains the principles and strategies I often share with them as well as many of their stories. I'll also share pieces of my own journey to illustrate different points.

How about you? You might not feel the need to scream, but are there areas where you feel frustrated or bottled up? Trapped by life's demands and high expectations—your own and others? Can you relate to those feelings of anger, fear, or pressure?

If so, I want to invite you to take seriously the questions *your* heart is asking. I'm talking about that small, too-easily ignored voice that refuses to give up on your aliveness. If you listen to that voice, you'll find that it is advocating for *you*. For the real you, the authentic you, the best version of you.

Learning to walk in aliveness is primarily about internal changes, not external changes. You don't necessarily have to quit your job, close your company, fire your board, sell your house, move to an exotic country, buy a yacht, take up skydiving, or anything else so dramatic. However, when you change on the inside, things often change on the outside. Those changes are up to you. You have full autonomy over the process.

This book is designed for leaders who want to pursue aliveness and are willing to do *whatever* it takes to make those changes happen. It is for people who are fully committed, who want to live with more purpose and passion, who desire to feel more alive every day. It is for those who are willing to question beliefs that are limiting them and make critical shifts that will catapult them into the best versions of themselves.

In the pages ahead, I will show you how to recognize, embrace, and increase your aliveness. I call this commitment to aliveness "Living All In." It's my life motto and the goal I strive to reach every day: to live fully engaged, fully alive, fully present. It's about making the most of the life I've been given.

Living All In is a lifestyle and a process, not a one-time decision or an instant change. That means you don't have to be in a hurry to fix everything all at once, but you do have to make a long-term commitment to keep discovering who you really are and how you can align your day-to-day experience with your authentic self.

You'll find that self-discovery is a circular process. You learn a little about yourself, so you lean into that and start to live it out. That new way of living, in turn, reveals more about yourself, which you then add to your tool kit and put into practice. That opens up even greater understanding and perspective, which expands your experience further...ad infinitum.

I'm going to warn you: the process can be messy. Even scary. It can be intimidating to be fully honest with yourself and with what you want and need in life. It can be challenging to consider what the pursuit of aliveness might mean for your schedule, your team, your family, your income. It can be difficult to accept this new version of you. You don't have to rush or force anything, but you do need to expect ambiguity, take your time, and—most importantly—commit to the journey.

These principles work. They produce results. It doesn't happen automatically or overnight, but if you focus on becoming more aware of yourself and more tenaciously devoted to the kind of life you want and need, things will change for the better.

As we begin, I invite you to make a commitment to yourself. Not to me, not to anyone around you, but to *you*.

Commit to honesty.

Commit to the process.

As you explore what your heart wants, and as you glimpse the thrill, energy, and fulfillment that aliveness offers, you'll need to be truthful with yourself and tenacious in your commitment to authenticity and alignment.

Aliveness starts with you.

Are you ready? Your journey starts now.

PART I

INTRODUCING ALIVENESS

(1)

THIS IS WHAT I WANT

Let me ask you a question. It's a simple question but an important one.

When have you felt most alive?

I don't mean "alive" in the biological sense. I mean alive on the inside. Truly alive. Fully alive. *Most alive.* I-never-want-this-feeling-to-end kind of alive.

Take a second to think about it. Is it when you're with your family? In nature? Closing a deal? Solving a problem? Traveling to new places? Riding a bike? Laughing with friends? Relaxing with your family? Making a difference in the world and giving back?

It might help to think back over your past, starting with your childhood. Can you remember specific moments when you felt fully, truly alive? Let your mind travel back over the years and reconnect with those memories, no matter how random or insignificant they might seem.

Maybe you took a family vacation to the beach, and to this day you remember the joy and love you felt then. Maybe that was a moment you felt truly alive.

Maybe you used to spend Saturday mornings at your grandmother's house, eating chocolate chip cookies and watching cartoons; that feeling of security and familiarity defined your childhood, and you felt alive.

Maybe you remember being in science class doing experiments, and you burned your eyebrows off because you mixed the wrong chemicals, but you loved how alive you felt when you experimented and explored.

Maybe you played sports, and you felt most alive when the game was on the line and you had the ball.

Maybe you remember feeling alive during your college years, when you were discovering who you are and learning to "adult" for the first time.

Maybe the moments of aliveness that you remember are more recent. It could have been at your job, when you discovered that you excelled in times of crisis, and you realized that you were made for this. Or maybe you took a trip somewhere with your friends, and you all laughed until you couldn't breathe, and you didn't want the feeling to ever end. Maybe your kids are little, and when you tuck them in you feel a deep rush of love, and for you, that is the very definition of being alive. Maybe it's a time you went skydiving, or a hike into the mountains alone, or a trip to a foreign country. Maybe it was when you fell in love. Maybe it was your wedding day. Maybe it was holding your baby for the first time.

Whenever or wherever it was, you found yourself saying, *Damn, this feels right! This feels like me. This is what I want. I wish it could be this way all the time.* Let me ask you a second question. As you think back on those specific moments of aliveness, *what does aliveness feel like to you?* In other words, if you could extract the essence from those moments and memories, what specific words would you use to describe it?

This is important because aliveness doesn't feel the same for everyone. If you're going to become more alive, you have to learn to identify, describe, and ultimately experience your own version of aliveness. So don't rush through this or skip over it. Take a minute and try to connect to those memories. Relive the emotions you experienced when you were there. Imagine how your body felt, what feelings were in your heart, what thoughts were in your mind. Try to recall the sensations in your body and in your emotions.

It's possible you've never stopped to think about this before, so be thoughtful as you answer. If you'd like, write it down in the space at the end of this chapter. Try to sum up your specific experience of aliveness in a few words. Whatever answer you write is the correct one. Just jot down whatever words come to mind to describe how aliveness feels in your body, your emotions, and your mind.

Over the years, I've asked my clients the same two questions:

1. When have you felt most alive?
2. What does aliveness feel like to you?

No two people have given me the same answer. Aliveness is unique because humans are unique, and no one can tell you exactly how, when, and why to feel most alive. There are common themes, but at the end of the day, we all experience life differently, and the words we choose to describe our best, most authentic, most satisfying moments are deeply personal. If you are having a hard time capturing the feeling, try describing it aspirationally.

For me, for example, aliveness feels like "giddy." That's an unusual word, maybe, but it's perfect for me. My senses are heightened, peace and satisfaction are at their peak, tension and fear have dissipated, and waves of joy and peace dominate my senses. There is an element of playful energy. It feels tingly, like electricity is coursing through my body.

Maybe for you, aliveness would feel more like calmness, adventure, rest, energy, peace, connection, significance, curiosity, generosity, freedom, thrill, love, joy, delight, gratitude, belonging, impact, or one of a thousand other words. That's why I started out by inviting you to explore what aliveness feels like to you. You get to describe it for yourself.

One of my clients described his feeling of aliveness as "like a kid getting out of bed on the first day of vacation." Another said it was like "being in the flow." Another said, "It feels like I live life on the balls of my feet, and I'm ready to jump." I love all of those descriptions.

As you connect to what makes you feel this way, it's possible that even the thought of your aliveness triggers a response in your body. You can imagine it and feel it all at once. It's energizing and invigorating.

Now ask yourself, *What if I could always feel that way, or feel that way more often? How would that change my life?*

Can you imagine that? Can you visualize a version of you that spends more time in aliveness than out of it?

I find that for many people, aliveness is a foreign concept because they've never been challenged to imagine a better quality of life than what they are experiencing. They have material and career goals, but those are superficial metrics of success. What about success on the inside? What about a lifestyle characterized by peace, joy, fulfillment, and positive energy? Some people seem to spend more time analyzing Amazon reviews for products they might buy than they do evaluating the quality of their own life. They're more concerned with choosing the right Netflix show than choosing a lifestyle that aligns with their values and priorities.

Take a moment to think not just about what aliveness feels like to you but about your *level* of aliveness. Do you regularly experience your personal definition of aliveness in your family; in your career and workplace; in your mental, emotional, and physical health; and in your friendships? Or do you have a sense that you're going through all the right motions but somehow life is eluding you? It's one thing to experience aliveness from time to time, but it's another to experience it as *a way of life* and in *all areas of your life*.

That brings us to the best part. This is the heart of this book, and I'll keep coming back to it.

You can take your personal version of aliveness into every aspect of your day-to-day life.

That might be hard to believe if you feel trapped and suppressed by circumstances beyond your control. I know the feeling. I've learned that you don't have to wait for anything around you to change before you feel more alive *because aliveness starts within you*. It's something you control, and you can choose to engage it in nearly any situation.

That doesn't mean that, in my case, I act giddy all the time. I don't have tingly feelings all day, every day. I don't walk around with a goofy smile on my face or ignore reality. It means I let that feeling, that experience of aliveness that I have defined for myself, become the filter and the frame for how I see the world. And when I do, I bring a better version of myself to my daily tasks.

In other words, aliveness is found at the intersection of *what makes you feel most alive* and *how you approach your day-to-day life*.

If either of those is out of whack—for example, if you don't know what aliveness feels like for you or your lifestyle isn't aligned with those things—then it will be hard or even impossible to experience ongoing aliveness. You'll be biologically alive, but you'll struggle to enjoy life to the fullest.

I know this from experience, as I'll share in the pages ahead. Not just mine, either, but that of hundreds of CEOs and other business leaders I've had the privilege of coaching. I'm so passionate about aliveness because the truths I'm going to share literally saved my life. I was fifty years old and on track to burn out, break down, or give up. I had resigned myself to the unsatisfying life I had rather than standing up for the life I really wanted.

That is, until I decided to do whatever it took to experience aliveness.

And then everything changed.

Today, I am a better leader, a better husband, a better father, and a better friend. I feel reborn. I have a new excitement about life, and I'm convinced the decades ahead will be the best of my life. The leaders I work with tell me my energy and passion are contagious.

That's what I want for everyone I meet. It's what I want for my wife and my kids. It's what I want for my friends. It's what I want for the leaders I coach.

And it's what I want for you.

I don't just want you to know *about* aliveness; I want you to *experience* it on a daily basis. I want you to learn how to take your personal brand of aliveness into your everyday life. I promise you, it will change everything.

So what, exactly, is aliveness? Here's my definition:

Aliveness is a state of being characterized by bringing the best version of yourself into your day-to-day experience through identifying and adopting mindsets and actions that align with your unique way of being fully alive.

It's a long definition, but it's important. Let's take a quick look at each phrase.

- *State of being* means aliveness is more than what you do or how you feel. It's how you exist and experience life. The goal isn't just to feel alive; it's to *be* alive.

- *The best version of yourself* refers to the fullest, most authentic, most fulfilled version of yourself. It's the "you" that is aligned with who you want to be and how you want to show up in life.
- *Day-to-day experience* means that aliveness is practical and present. It should influence every area of your life, every day of your life, in any situation or circumstance.
- *Identifying and adopting the mindsets and actions* is all about the process of finding what works for you. It's about alignment with how you experience being alive. This means you've got some work to do. This is *your* aliveness. If you want it, you have to start by defining it. Your mindsets and actions should promote aliveness, not block it, which means you have to understand what makes you tick and be willing to change things that are misaligned.
- Finally, *that align with your unique way of being fully alive* points to the process of shifting your inner and outer worlds to create better alignment. You have a distinctive way of experiencing aliveness, and your goal is to align your mindsets and actions with that experience. You'll spend the rest of your life getting better and better at this because you are a *complex* person and a *changing* person.

If you haven't done so already, I encourage you to write down your answers to the questions I asked above. You can use the space below if you'd like. These are just your initial thoughts, so don't worry about getting your wording exactly right at this point. We're going to be refining it as we move through the book, so this is just the starting line, not the finish.

1. I have felt most alive when I ... (write down three examples)

2. For me, aliveness feels like _____ in my body.

3. What pictures and images of me (and others) best reflect when I am feeling alive?

4. How often do I feel authentically alive in my day-to-day life? How many times do I feel this way per day or week, and for how many hours or minutes?

5. What if I could feel aliveness more often? How would that change my life?

2

THE CIRCLE OF ALIVENESS

I LOVE RIDING MY BIKE AND EXERCISING. I'VE COMPETED IN OVER SIXTY triathlons in my life, and even though I live in Chicago, I ride outdoors over 250 days a year. I'm not an engineer, but I have first-hand experience with the basic physics that go into making a bike work. Let's think it through for a moment.

To get started, you apply force to one pedal, then the other, and so on. That creates torque, which is transferred through the chain to the rear wheel. This results in something called "angular momentum," which propels the bike forward. In other words, those small, relatively easy movements of your legs are transformed into strong forward motion.

You probably know from experience that as the wheels spin faster, the bicycle becomes more stable and the ride is smoother. That's because the gyroscopic effect brings stability and inertia, similar to a top. Once you get going, you can even coast and enjoy the wind in your face, all while traveling toward your destination.

It's simple science. To a child learning how to ride a bike, they likely aren't thinking about the science. They are only focused on keeping their feet on the pedals and having their hands on the handlebars to steer.

Of course, if you use words like *torque* and *angular momentum* with a child, they'll look at you with a blank stare and change the subject to dog breath or their itchy socks. For kids (and honestly, for all of us), learning to ride a bike is mostly about how it *feels*. You can try to explain it all you want, but a child won't learn how to ride a bike by listening to a lecture.

Kids learn by doing it. They learn by feeling it. They have to figure out the right mix of balance, speed, and risk. They have to try, tip over, and try again. They have to find the courage to go fast enough and far enough for the physics to kick in.

At first it feels unnatural. They need you to run alongside them, gasping for air, trying to keep them from falling over or running you over. Then, suddenly, there comes a moment when it all works. They just *get* it. They can't explain it, but they feel it, and off they go. Then they leave you in the dust, because bikes move faster than feet and take a lot less effort. You watch from a distance, and the wonder on their face (mixed with terror, at first) makes it all worthwhile for both of you.

The model I want to present to you is simple, like riding a bicycle. It might seem a little complicated at first, as I discuss the moving parts, but in reality, it is less about the parts themselves and more about what happens when they come together and function as a whole.

The goal here isn't to have a theoretical understanding of everything *before* you start but rather to be inspired *to start*. As you go, as you catch what aliveness feels like, you won't need to think about all the moving parts as much.

It might feel a little unnatural at first. That's normal. You've spent years, even decades living a certain way, and trying out a new framework and new mindsets can make you feel wobbly. But soon, you'll just get it. It will make sense.

After that, the horizon is the limit. I'm not saying you won't have some terror mixed into the wonder, but the wonder will win out. And once you know what aliveness feels like and what it does for you, it becomes something you never forget.

Just like riding a bike.

We're going to explore the different parts of the aliveness model throughout this book, but I think it would be helpful to give you an overview before we get started.

When I work with people to become more alive, I don't give them numbered steps. I don't give them a flowchart. I don't give them a list of keys, principles, or secrets to success. I'm not criticizing those things, but I don't think aliveness can be packaged that neatly.

Instead, I listen to them, I learn from them, and I try to help them look within themselves to find what's been there all along: their aliveness. In every conversation, I have the same goal. What is the next step this person can take toward aliveness? Often, it's removing layers that unconsciously block them from feeling alive, such as unproductive judgments and beliefs.

My goal is not to give you a one-size-fits-all model that is guaranteed to make you fully alive in thirty days. Instead, my goal is to give you the tools you need to find your own aliveness, which is going to be a journey that is as unique and nuanced as you are.

As I put together my experiences and thoughts for this book, I even struggled to come up with a diagram that accurately represents what aliveness means for me and for the incredible business leaders I've had the privilege of coaching. Reducing aliveness to a chart or a diagram seems limiting, even inadequate. It's like trying to explain what it's like to fall in love, to hear a symphony, or to taste a five-star meal.

So, while I'll do my best to lay out what I believe will help you achieve it, I do so with humility. This isn't an instruction manual as much as it is me holding the handlebars of your bike for a short time. I'm here to give you a little guidance and support, but you have to figure out aliveness for yourself. I can run only so far before my age or my lunch catches up with me, but you are the one who has to keep going.

I remember working with Cindy,[1] an executive vice president for a consulting firm who was in the midst of a job transition in her fifties. She felt out of control. She told me the task of figuring out what was next seemed like scaling a mountain or boiling the ocean.

I asked her, "How do you want the experience to feel?"

She thought about it and said, "Like a map."

I said, "And who are you?

Cindy responded, "An explorer."

We talked for a while about how an explorer approaches life with curiosity, courage, and passion. She was determined to make that her mindset as she explored what role would get her most excited.

I loved that analogy. I'd like to suggest that you adopt the same view as you approach aliveness. You're going to be learning ways of thinking and acting that might seem unfamiliar, but that's the whole point: you're exploring what it means to be truly you.

Only you can decide what to do with the map called life. Only you can choose what to change, what to pursue, what to learn, what to say no to, and what to say yes to.

So if something I say doesn't resonate with you, that's okay. Make the model of aliveness that I'm going to share your own. Cross things out, scribble in the margins, tear out pages, do whatever you need to do to get there. It's your journey, and I think you're going to love it.

Circle of Aliveness

Let's begin by understanding the model of aliveness that we'll explore in the next chapters.

For me, aliveness is best represented by a circle. After that long introduction I just gave, you might have expected something more complicated. And to be honest, when I first went through the process of distilling everything down to its core, what I came up with *was* more complicated. I had multiple pages covered with flywheels, gears, bridges, paths, boxes, and arrows.

But the more I looked at it, the more I realized I was explaining too much. Aliveness is less about telling and more about showing. It's less about you watching how I do it and more about you trying it out for yourself.

So now it's a circle.

A circle of aliveness.

A circle centered on what I call your Optimal State.

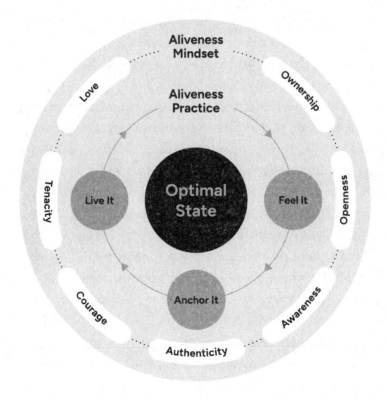

I'll explain what the terms in this diagram mean as we go along. But before we get started, let's talk about why your aliveness looks like a circle.

First, because *circles don't have a start or an end, and neither does your journey toward aliveness.* You've always been alive, and you've always pursued greater aliveness, even when you didn't have words for it. All you're doing is focusing your efforts and learning to balance while you gain momentum. Your experience of aliveness started when you were born, and it won't end until your time on earth is done.

Second, because *circles are completely connected, and so are you.* A circle is a holistic, integrated shape, which is the nature of aliveness. It's the only geometric shape where every point along the shape is the same distance from the center. Every part is as close as possible to every other part. That's how your life should be—integrated, connected, and close.

Third, because *circles imply cycles, and aliveness means ongoing effort and growth.* Just as wheels and gears get their power from rotating over and over, so your growth in aliveness gets its power from your ongoing work to explore it and expand it. You're playing the long game here. The more you learn, the more you'll grow, and the more you'll grow, the more you'll keep learning. It's a cycle that moves you forward and upward.

Finally, because *circles can group many elements together into one integrated whole.* We're going to walk through a number of individual principles and elements that contribute to aliveness, but don't lose sight of the fact that they are all contained within the one goal of aliveness. That means you can work on them as you see fit and when you feel able, and you can be confident that every investment you make is contributing to the overall vision of becoming more alive.

Inner Circle: Optimal State

The first circle, the center of the whole shebang, is what I call your *Optimal State*, or OS. This represents the bull's-eye of how we want to feel and what we want our daily experience to be. This is the goal and the intention behind all we do.

Remember, aliveness is a state of being. It's when you bring the best version of yourself into your day-to-day experience through identifying and adopting mindsets and actions that align with what makes you feel most alive. So when you live with aliveness—that is, when you experience aliveness on an ongoing, regular basis across every area—you are in your Optimal State.

This state is highly individualized, as I mentioned in chapter 1. It's *your* experience. It's *your* unique brand or flavor of aliveness. We're not just talking about general principles of aliveness; we're talking about how, when, and why *you* feel most alive.

Your Optimal State is you at your best. Not somebody else's best, not someone else's expectation of you, not some idealized image you might have had of yourself, but your *true and authentic* best. It's the version of you that is aligned inside and out, that experiences life fully and brings its entire self to everything.

Your goal is to spend as much time in this place as possible. It's to approach everything in life—the good, the bad, and the ugly—from that place of inner aliveness. That's what I mean by bringing the best version of yourself into your day-to-day experiences.

We'll discuss Optimal State in much more detail in part 4, where I will share about how to discover, define, and expand it, but I'll also refer to the concept throughout the book, especially when I describe the experiences of different clients I've worked with.

Middle Circle: Aliveness Practice

Now, let's add a circle. This next circle represents your *Aliveness Practice*.

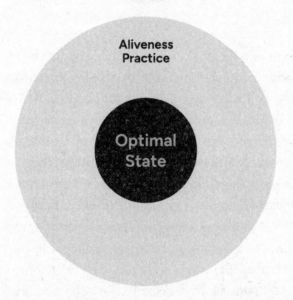

Why do I call it a practice? Because you can't just snap your fingers and magically exist in a nirvana of aliveness. It doesn't work that way. To experience aliveness takes a great deal of work. And it's not a onetime thing. You'll need to practice this on a continual basis.

The practice I'm referring to is the work of alignment. This circle illustrates the ongoing process of aligning three things that together create aliveness and allow you to remain in your Optimal State:

- the way you *feel*
- the way you *think*
- the way you *live*

Like the inner circle, this middle circle is intensely personal and practical. This is where I spend most of my time when I'm working with leaders, and it's where progress is the most exciting.

In part 3, we'll take a closer look at Aliveness Practice. We'll talk about how you are propelled or hindered by the ways you feel, think, and act. We'll dive into how you experience aliveness. We'll explore ways to identify your Anchoring Mindsets, which are the primary keys to alignment. Finally, we'll look at ways you can intentionally accelerate your process toward aliveness and how you can recognize and remove what is blocking you from achieving it.

Outer Circle: Aliveness Mindset

Finally, let's add one last circle, which I call your *Aliveness Mindset*.

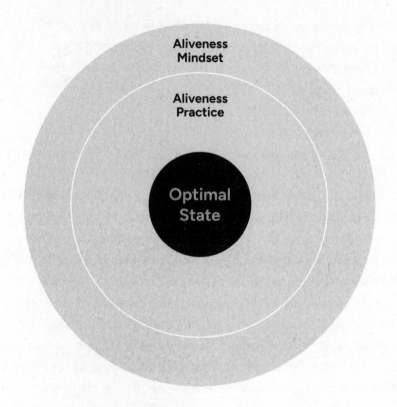

This circle consists of seven individual mindsets that together form one overarching philosophy or approach to life: an Aliveness Mindset.

A mindset refers to how your brain develops and maintains your unique perspective. It is the beliefs and attitudes that shape the lens you see the world "through". Mindset guides your behavior, helps you choose your priorities, direct your decisions, and leads you to set and pursue your goals.

The seven mindsets are

- Ownership
- Openness
- Awareness
- Authenticity

- Courage
- Tenacity
- Love

Together, these are the entry points for aliveness, because without these things, it will be nearly impossible to stay in your Optimal State. You don't have to master them before you begin to experience aliveness. That would be impossible, because we're all works in progress. But you will find, as you go, that you'll need all of them in different moments.

You'll also find that you *grow* in them. The pursuit of aliveness is not linear, but circular and cyclical. The more you take *ownership*, for example, the more you'll need to be *open*. The more open you are, the more aware you *become*. The more aware you become, the more *honesty*, *courage*, and *tenacity* you need.

And so it goes. On and on, back and forth, around and around, as each new understanding makes you a more authentic, more alive version of yourself.

Putting It All Together

Putting the three circles in terms of our biking example, the outer circle, *Aliveness Mindset*, describes the basic, essential ways of thinking that you need to climb on the bike, kick off from the curb, and wobble and feel your way toward freedom.

The middle circle, *Aliveness Practice*, is the ongoing effort and skill you apply to keep moving, faster and faster, toward whatever destination you choose. This is the act of pedaling, and each movement becomes momentum that pushes you forward.

And *Optimal State*? That's the reward. That's the wind in your face and the fresh air filling your lungs. That's the rush of living, of exploring, or sailing into an unknown future with the certainty that you're taking your best self wherever you go.

Here is the Circle of Aliveness again. Notice that two of these circles are made up of multiple components, which we'll explore in more detail in their respective chapters.

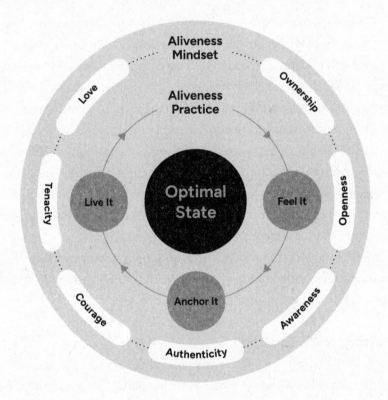

Once you figure out the dynamics of pedaling and steering and balance, the bike does the hard work of moving you forward. You just push down on whichever pedal is at the top, and the chains and gears take care of the rest. The actions are simple, rhythmic, even relaxing. I'm not saying it's always easy, but as long as you move your feet in circles and control the balance and steering, the bike does the hard work of making progress.

That's how aliveness works too. Once you really get going, your own aliveness does the hard work of carrying you forward. You have to steer, and you have to balance, and you have to keep pedaling by nudging each area of your life forward, but you are propelled and carried by the momentum that comes from within you.

In the next chapter, I'm going to share parts of my own aliveness journey to illustrate the power and potential of aliveness. My story is somewhat dramatic, at least when it comes to my career. Everyone's story is different, and you don't need to do what I did or go through what I went through.

But I can say with all my heart, it was worth it. I believe it will be for you too. It was a defining moment in my life, and I'm proud of how I handled it. I learned a lot about what works. This book includes many of those insights in an effort to help you find the most impactful steps to take.

1. Think of a specific situation that is very challenging for you: maybe a work problem, a relational conflict, or a tough decision. How do you want to experience this challenge? How are you currently handling it? (For example: "I'm reactive; I'm blaming myself or others.") If you could choose to show up in this situation in a specific way, what would it be? ("I'd be more open or curious." "I'd ask more questions." "I would be more decisive." Etc.)

2. What is the next step you could take toward making that desired experience a reality? If you aren't sure of your next step, you might want to consider the advice you would give to your best friend with the same problem.

Note: Your next step is an agreement you are making with yourself. If the issue seems big, break it down into small steps that are easily attainable. I call these "hop over the fence" goals. Set yourself up for success.

3

MORE THAN A NICE CONCEPT

On a practical level, is aliveness all that important? Or is it just a luxury, a nice but unrealistic concept? If you have food to eat and a roof over your head, if you have family and friends, and if you are relatively healthy and safe from harm, shouldn't that be enough?

I've talked to many CEOs and other leaders who express a similar thought. They aren't necessarily satisfied with their lives, but they feel guilty asking for more because they are aware that they are privileged and blessed. And it's true—they have a lot to be grateful for. So do I. So do you.

But that doesn't mean we can't expect more or receive more. The human capacity to enjoy life is enormous. Almost infinite. Why settle for less than full aliveness? Especially when the things that block aliveness are within our power to address.

In a moment we're going to look at several reasons why aliveness is important, but first, let's think about what a *lack* of aliveness looks like. When I talk with people who are not experiencing the level of aliveness they would like, they often describe themselves in one or more of the following ways. See if you can relate to any of these.

- They feel **stagnant or trapped**. They might have a title, income, or influence, but these things feel like golden handcuffs, locking them into a world that seems more stifling than they imagined it would be.

- They spend most of their time and energy **doing what they _have_ to do**, not what they _wish_ they could do. That usually means attending innumerable meetings and answering never-ending emails.

- When they look at their to-do list, their **energy goes down**, not up. Their meetings and appointments are more about putting out fires than conquering new territory. The magic has faded, and they no longer look forward to the workday.

- They are **frustrated** with their own decision-making process. They put off decisions out of fatigue, insecurity, or uncertainty, and they wish they had a better set of criteria to guide their choices.

- They thought they would be happier than they are by now. They assumed financial success or career advancement would create a more satisfying life, but something seems to be **missing**.

I can relate to every single one of the above scenarios. That was the way I ran my life for the two decades when I ran my company. My fixed, reactive mindset resulted in feeling drained, frustrated, unfulfilled, and unhappy at work. Even worse, that leaked into every area of my life. My family and friendships were affected, and so was my mental and emotional health.

Something inside me knew it wasn't enough, though. I knew life was capable of being better than that, and I wanted to discover how. I wanted to feel more energy, not less energy. I wanted to spend my time being strategic and creative, not checking off a to-do list. I wanted to have a big impact, not just a big paycheck. That was the catalyst for my own aliveness journey, which I'll share a little later.

For many people I've talked to, frustration, disappointment, entrapment, and disillusionment are the status quo or the baseline. They might experience flashes of aliveness at times, but those are the exception, not the rule. They are living, but they aren't experiencing aliveness. Not in the sense they could be. And on some level, they know it.

Do *you* know it?

Is there something within you that is telling you there must be more?

Take a moment to write down anything you feel frustrated with, trapped by, or disappointed in. Writing out a list like this might feel negative, even discouraging, but there's a reason for this exercise. You can't step into greater aliveness until you identify the ways in which you are *not* alive. Think of this as a self-assessment tool, not just a pity-me list. Be honest with yourself and give yourself permission to complain. To whine. To bitch a little. Nobody else is going to read this unless you show them, so don't censor yourself.

1. What am I most frustrated or disappointed with right now? What is missing?

2. Do I feel trapped by any of my responsibilities or by the expectations of others? Do I spend a lot of time fulfilling obligations? Which ones are the most difficult to carry? (List them here.)

3. Looking at my calendar for the past two weeks and the upcoming two weeks, what things consistently drain my energy and motivation? What do I dread doing or find myself avoiding?

4. If I could change two to three things in my life today with a magic wand, what would they be?

Listing your frustrations, disillusionments, disappointments, and obligations might feel negative, but it's a step in a positive direction. Why? Because you are admitting to yourself that you don't want to maintain the status quo forever. Awareness is the first step toward drawing a line in the sand and saying, "I'm not okay with this. I can't keep going this way. Something needs to change."

I'm not saying that every frustration you experience is due to a lack of aliveness. If you're upset because you had a flat tire on the way to work and had to reschedule your entire morning, that's normal. That's just life being unpredictable. But on the other hand, if the flat tire triggered deep-seated anger because it reminded you how much you resent the stress of your job, or if you spiraled into anxiety because you were operating with no margin and this was the last straw, then maybe even that roadside frustration is trying to tell you something.

When you feel trapped, disillusioned, or angry—especially if that feeling has lasted for a long time—it might be your inner voice's way of telling you it's time to make some changes. That kind of reactivity is often a symptom of a deeper dissatisfaction or an underlying mindset of fear or anxiety.

Often, our inner pain is what drives us to change. It shouldn't necessarily be that way, but it is. It's the same dynamic that frequently happens with our physical bodies. We get some aches and pains, we get a checkup, and the doctor tells us seventeen things we could do to improve our quality of life. We could have been doing those seventeen things already—but we waited until we felt enough discomfort to motivate us to change.

When it comes to aliveness, I find that many people (me included) discover it only after enduring a non-alive lifestyle for so long that it has worn them down. They manage to get by for a while because they are strong, determined people with a high tolerance for discomfort, but that can last for only so long. As they grow more unhappy, and as they become more aware of their "unaliveness," they finally engage in a level of soul-searching that leads them to make the changes needed to align their lives with the things that truly produce aliveness.

Let me share an example. Jerry is a CEO who was in business with a partner, but they didn't really speak to each other anymore. Over the last decade they had drifted apart, each immersed in their roles without any real interaction. The business was profitable, but Jerry was unhappy and frustrated, and he had felt that way for a decade. He had finally reached the point where he was unwilling to tolerate the status quo.

When our coaching sessions began, I asked him what he really wanted from the business (more joy) and his business partner (alignment on succession, strategy, and compensation), what responsibility he had for the current dysfunction (he has been avoiding initiating the difficult conversations), and whether he was willing to take whatever action was necessary to find more happiness and meaning at work (he was).

The following week he reached out to his partner to attempt improving their relationship. The partner refused to discuss the topics he suggested. Jerry had the courage and firmness to give his partner an ultimatum. "Either I buy you out, you buy me out, or we fold the company." His vision of enjoying work overcame his resistance to potential conflict.

You don't have to wait a decade before you make a change. Aliveness isn't a last-gasp way to avoid complete burnout. You can start living this way at any time. With your physical body, you can make proactive choices to eat right, exercise, and rest; in the same way, with your internal self, you can decide to pursue aliveness right now, regardless of where you find yourself.

Once you catch a vision for aliveness as a way of life, you'll pursue it for its own sake. You'll see who you could truly be—the best version of yourself—and you'll strive to bring that version of yourself into everything you experience. And when you do, you'll wonder how you ever managed to live any other way.

We've seen some of the negative consequences of not experiencing aliveness; let's approach the topic from a more positive angle. Why should you pursue aliveness? What good is it? Why should it matter to you? Why is it more than a luxury, more than just a nice thought or an ideal?

1. Because you deserve it.

This is often hard for high-performing people to accept. You're probably used to being the giver, not the taker. You're the protector, the provider, the hero, the martyr. You might not be comfortable thinking in terms of what you deserve, because you understand how quickly that can devolve into narcissism. If anything, you're likely all too aware of why you *don't* deserve to pursue the things that make you most alive.

Here's the thing. By "deserve" I don't mean you've earned aliveness because you've worked hard and done everything right. That might be true, but you deserve to feel alive, fulfilled, satisfied, and complete simply because you're human. Because you exist. Because you are here. You don't have to do anything to earn that. It's something every human needs and should aspire to.

If you've conditioned yourself to always postpone the things that make you feel most alive because that's how you're "supposed" to live, I'd like to suggest that you rethink your mentality. You have a need, a capacity, and a right to get the most out of the life you've been given.

I'm not suggesting you make happiness your one and only goal in life or that you hurt other people just to get what you want. Not at all. I'm simply saying that you don't have to choose between being the responsible, hardworking, faithful, and effective person you strive to be *and* being truly alive.

You can have both. You need to have both. You deserve to have both.

That may seem selfish, but it's not. We will talk about why in another chapter, but centering yourself in this process is an act of generosity to yourself *and* to those around you.

2. Because it will improve every area of your life in a holistic, integrated way.

Aliveness isn't something you add to your life, like a hobby or an area of knowledge. Remember, aliveness is bringing the best version of yourself into your day-to-day experience of life. It's more than what you do: it's how you think and live. Aliveness reconnects the fragments of you and brings them into alignment and congruence. It's holistic and all-encompassing.

Aliveness digs deep into the essence of you in order to bring the real you to the surface, and that has positive repercussions in every facet of your life, not just in your professional world. I hear this from my clients time and time again. This holistic aspect is why the Living All In practice isn't just a business coaching tool or a leadership development tool. It includes those things, but it's more than that. It's a way of existing in the world, and that goes far beyond your job.

Because aliveness affects all the parts of you, it isn't something you can just switch on. It's not like a setting on your phone that you can enable and instantly have access to the fullest version of you. Rather, becoming more alive is like a series of cycles or interconnected actions. Everything you do to improve has a ripple effect on everything else.

Have you ever tried to carry a couch or bedframe into a house and up a flight of stairs? At a certain point in life, you realize it's not worth it and you hire a moving company. But I'm assuming that at least once, you opted to do it yourself. You couldn't do it alone, so you enlisted someone to help. You quickly discovered that every time one of you lifted a corner, it affected all the other corners. The weight was only part of the battle: the real challenge was figuring out how to "pivot!" as you maneuvered the bulky, wobbly thing through doorways, up the stairs, and around corners. It was less about brute strength and more about coordination.[2]

That's a bit how aliveness works. It's not that you have to exert superhuman effort to make it happen. It's more like you have to pay attention to different parts of your life and learn how they work together. When you improve your work life, for example, you will likely see improvements in your physical and mental health. As you improve your health, you reap benefits in your family relationships. If your family life is healthy, you are able to be a better boss at work.

Living things need to be connected in order to flourish. They need an open flow of nutrients, oxygen, and even waste in order to stay healthy. We understand this on a natural level: plants, animals, and the human body function this way. Apply that same truth to the inorganic parts of your life: your actions, interests, relationships, goals, and more. The more you can connect those things and allow for a free flow of energy and resources between them, the more efficient and effective you will be, and the more alive you will feel.

Aliveness is crucial because it counteracts the unhealthy human tendency to silo things: work, family, sleep, leisure, and so on. It reminds you that you are a complex, interconnected system of parts—and they all matter. They all affect each other. With each step you take to identify and adopt ways of thinking and acting that are aligned with what makes you feel most alive, you improve every other area, and you bring the best version of yourself into everything you do.

3. Because the people in your world want and need you to experience it.

It's important to note that aliveness is never just about you. You are connected to other people in so many ways, and your interactions and relationships with others will have a direct effect on your experience of life as well as theirs. When you bring the best version of yourself to your day-to-day experiences, it is likely to create better connections for you *and* those you relate to.

In their 2023 book *The Good Life,* authors Robert Waldinger and Marc Schulz share research and findings that could be considered a road map to happiness. In particular, they highlight the importance of good relationships as the most significant principle for leading a fulfilling life. Their book is based on a famous longitudinal Harvard study that spanned eighty-five years and involved multiple generations of researchers and participants. The study examined the essential elements contributing to human flourishing and examined the interplay between relationships, careers, health, and personal development to better understand what factors might foster happiness and well-being. Waldinger and Schulz conclude, "Good relationships keep us healthier and happier. Period."[3]

One of the things I often share with people is the positive secondary effect their aliveness will have on their loved ones and others who are around them. Doesn't that hold true for you? The people closest to you don't want you to be unhappy. They don't want you to be a martyr. They want you to be the best version of yourself, and your decision to become that person and to live in a state of fulfillment is in their best interests, not just yours.

Too often we think in zero-sum terms when it comes to aliveness. *If I pursue what I want,* we might think, *it means I have to sacrifice what my family wants, and they will see me as a selfish person. If I give my employees what they need, I have to suffer the lack of something I need.*

That's simply not true, or at least it's not a given. If you are committed to both being healthy and to serving other people in a healthy way, you'll usually find solutions that benefit everyone. I call this "finding option C." When you are healthy, you are better equipped to use your gifts to help others. That's why genuine happiness, satisfaction, joy, and fulfillment have a way of lifting other people up, not pulling them down. Your family, friends, and employees need you to be as healthy and happy as possible.

4. Because today matters.

One of the toxic lies of "success," as our society often defines it, is that happiness lies on the other side of the next achievement. The next deal, the next sale, the next bonus, the next acquisition, the next product launch, the next million, the next accolade, the next relationship, the next stage of life.

It's the proverbial pot of gold at the end of the rainbow, though—always just out of reach. You find yourself struggling, striving, and stressing in an attempt to reach something, only to get it and discover that it's fun for a moment, but it cannot create lasting peace or fulfillment. In psychology, this is often called the hedonic treadmill.

I'm not saying that goals don't matter. I love goals. I'm a goal-oriented person. Reaching goals gives you a wonderful sense of satisfaction. But that satisfaction tends to leak, and it happens very quickly after you get what you were chasing. So while goals are an essential *part* of life, they cannot be the *point* of your life or you'll always be pursuing what's next and never find a level of fulfillment that transcends what you do.

I'm also not saying that plans don't matter. You should definitely plan for the future, but don't neglect today in the name of planning for tomorrow. Don't wait to enjoy life until you're retired. Don't wait to spend time with your kids. Don't wait to laugh with your spouse. Don't wait to congratulate yourself for a job well done. Don't wait to spend money. Don't wait to be generous. Don't wait to travel, to learn, to experience, to *live*.

In *The Good Life*, Waldinger and Schulz describe a dynamic they call "time famine," which is the feeling that there is insufficient time in a day to live the life we desire. Paradoxically, we often hold on to a belief that, in some unspecified future, there will be a miraculous "time surplus," where we will be less overwhelmed, less rushed, and less burdened, which will finally allow us to fully enjoy the life we crave. The problem with this mentality is that we tend to postpone activities that bring us happiness and make us feel most alive because we are waiting for an imaginary and often unattainable surplus of time.[4]

We were not meant to hang our happiness on some future achievement. We can't go back to the past, and we can't live in the future. We have only been given the present. We only have today.

That means *today* matters most.

One of the greatest benefits of aliveness is the freedom to simply enjoy today, with all its imperfections, all its uncertainties, all its ambiguity. Yesterday is gone and tomorrow isn't guaranteed, but you have today. Why not live it to the fullest?

o o o

We've looked at four reasons you should make aliveness a priority:

- You deserve it and need it.
- It transforms your entire self from the inside out.
- Your friends, loved ones, employees, and clients need you to be the best version of yourself.
- Today is all you've got, so you might as well enjoy it.

Any one of those reasons would be convincing enough, but when you take them together, you can see that aliveness is much more than just a nice thought or an idealistic dream.

Aliveness is a need built into the very fiber of your being, and it's something that will influence your health, happiness, and longevity. That's why the journey toward aliveness is a worthwhile one. It isn't always easy, but like leg day at the gym or getting a good night's sleep, the results are worth the momentary discomfort.

You need it, you deserve it, and you'll thrive as you walk into it.

1. Allow yourself to dream and think of what the benefits and impact of feeling more alive would be.

2. What do you see as your biggest challenge to embracing aliveness?

3. What is one thing you could do today to invest in your aliveness? If you can't think of anything right now, that's okay. Try to make your action aspirational.

(4)

SHOW UP OR SHUT UP

I SPENT THE LAST CHAPTER EMPHASIZING THE NEED FOR ALIVENESS for two reasons. First, because we often don't realize what aliveness even is. And second, because *we often don't choose to pursue it.*

I know this from personal experience. As I shared in the introduction, I had an epiphany in April of 2012 that I needed to figure out how to become truly alive. And yet it took me well over two years to leave my role as a CEO of a large company and become an executive coach for high-performing leaders.

It was the scariest career move I've ever made.

It was also the best one. After much soul-searching and personal growth, I had come to realize it was what I had to do in order to be true to myself and my aliveness. That's not the case with most people, but it was with me. Today, I am beyond grateful that I found the clarity and courage to pursue a path that was aligned with aliveness.

The clarity and courage didn't happen overnight. This is what I want you to see, because your own journey with aliveness won't either. The time and effort you put into understanding who you are and what you want is an essential part of the process. Only you can understand you, but to get there, you have put in the work.

For me, the journey started by screaming, but several years passed after that before I pivoted in my career. Those years were necessary for me to dig deep into my own heart and mind. I had to understand not only my own frustration but the reasons I was resisting unhappiness instead of listening to it.

It was a messy process but an exhilarating one. In the years since, I've seen those same two things—messiness and exhilaration—hold true for the majority of my clients. As we close this introductory section and prepare to explore the Aliveness Circle, which represents your aliveness journey, I'd like to share a few highlights from my own journey. Not because it's "better" or "right" but because it illustrates the necessity of messy exhilaration, and I think it will help set your expectations for what the process might involve for you.

Thinking back to April 2012, I'll never forget the feeling of excitement I had when I came home from the retreat and saw my wife, Judy. I had left for the retreat feeling heavy, isolated, and without hope for improving or getting what I wanted. I returned feeling lighter and more alive. I had released pent-up emotions, thoughts, and wants. I saw opportunities and options where before I had seen only dead ends. I recognized a path to happiness where I previously felt one didn't exist.

I joined the leadership group Jim and Diana led, where they taught a leadership model called the 15 Commitments of Conscious Leadership. I became a founding member. The deal was this: every leader had to be willing to risk *everything* for their aliveness. Risk our comfort. Risk our jobs. Risk our relationships if they are no longer serving us. Risk our income. Risk our security. We had to commit to overcoming any blocks to our full aliveness. I needed to shift my mindsets to become the person I wanted to be and to feel more alive. It soon became clear that aliveness, for me, meant that I needed my work to have an impact and to be exciting to me. That was a problem because my work was draining me, not making me feel more alive.

Unfortunately, I didn't believe that I could just quit. I was the CEO of a business my father had started and led for fifty years before he passed away unexpectedly in 2000. I felt like the business was my connection to him. Plus, my two siblings were my partners. We had worked alongside each other for almost twenty years. They were supportive and hardworking, and I trusted them, and they trusted me. But I knew if I left the business, it would probably close. Neither of them wanted to run it. I wrestled with that decision for more than two years. It was a difficult, painful time, and the longer I held on to my position, the worse I felt.

In the meantime, something interesting began to happen.

I was changing on the inside as I incorporated principles of aliveness in my home life and at work. Customers and friends noticed that I seemed happier, more present, more engaged. As a natural result of my inner changes, I began sharing stories with my family, friends, and customers about everything I was learning and applying in my life. Often, days later, those people would call me or text me to say I had helped them with their own issues.

Every time I heard that, I felt a buzz in my body. I lit up. I felt alive.

I was more and more frustrated running the business, but I was discovering a hidden talent for encouraging and coaching leaders. Not only did I enjoy telling people about what I was learning, I was good at it, and they received value from what I shared with them. Between my leadership trainings and my years as a CEO, I knew how to guide leaders toward their goals and help them experience greater satisfaction. I got my coaching certification and began to take on a few clients in the evenings and on weekends.

And yet I struggled to make the switch in my full-time career. Primarily out of fear, I tried to keep one foot in the family business and one foot in coaching. Eventually that became untenable. Within a year, some close friends and mentors had called me out on my fear. They told in no uncertain terms that I was my own obstacle, and if I didn't get the hell out of the way, nothing was ever going to change.

I had to show up or shut up. It was time to do what I had known I needed to do, deep inside, for a long time. I decided to step away from my role as CEO.

First, I talked to my siblings. That conversation was a major step, and it was a shock to them. It was emotional. It was painful. But it was necessary. After a long period of planning, we began to wind down the business. The process was well-executed and neat. And it was also messy as hell. On September 30, 2015, the company officially closed its doors. I felt a lot of emotions: sadness, fear, and joy. I mourned the employees I would miss, the connection to my father I felt every day at work, the emotional weight of ending a sixty-five-year-old company.

I also allowed myself to get excited about the next chapter, despite my fear that I might not find professional and financial success as an executive coach. I let myself dream about a future that was aligned with who I was and the kind of life I wanted rather than shoehorning myself into the expectations of others or the demands of my day-to-day schedule.

Three years after screaming at that retreat and realizing I was angry and unhappy, I had finally understood the path I needed to take and—just as importantly—given myself permission to follow it.

The first year of full-time coaching was both exhilarating and terrifying, kind of like that five-year-old riding a bike for the first time. I had a lot to learn. I still do. That's never going to end. But even with the ups and downs, I was a thousand times more excited, passionate, and engaged than I had been before. I had found my own Optimal State, my own version of aliveness, and I was learning to live there regardless of my circumstances.

Today, nearly a decade into my practice, I can confidently say it was the best decision I have ever made. I feel more alive and fulfilled than ever. My clients and other people who meet me and hear about what I do can sense it in my enthusiastic energy. I've watched the same dynamic occur for countless other leaders I've coached. I've seen person after person, boardroom after board-room, and company after company transformed through the power of aliveness.

I don't share these details to boast or to convince you that your journey should look like mine. I just want to illustrate how alive-ness is found within you, and your path forward is an extension of the things you've learned and understood until this point.

I didn't do it all the right way, because there was no right way to do it. I had to make peace with that. If you've ignored your authentic self for fifty years like I did, you're going to make some waves when you correct your course. I had waited a very long time to stand up and speak up, and that caused hurt that I could have diminished if I had only given myself permission to be more honest during the twenty years leading up to that moment.

That's part of the reason for this book. I don't want you to wait too long to become yourself. I don't want you to have to move heaven and earth just to fix what you could have avoided breaking in the first place.

You shouldn't have to quit your job or damage important relationships or jeopardize your retirement plans to be fully alive. Few, if any, of the many business leaders I've coached have changed careers in their pursuit of aliveness. But you will have to be tenacious. You will have to be brave, wise, strong, and creative. You will have to take some risks. You will have to have a few hard conversations and maybe even disappoint some people—at least at first. You will have to look inward to discover the aliveness within you. That may or may not include screaming—that part is up to you. But you have to be willing to pursue aliveness wherever it takes you.

I'm here to tell you that you'll be glad you did. No, the journey has not always been easy, but it's been exciting, and it's been healthy, and it's been fruitful. I wouldn't change it for anything.

You know what I would change if I could go back? I'd pay less attention to fear. I'd be less swayed by the expectations of others. I'd believe in myself more. And I'd give myself more grace to fail and space to grow.

I can't go back and do those things. But I can go *forward* that way. And so can you.

---

1. Have you had any "epiphany" moments where you realized things could not continue as they were? How did you feel? What allowed you to take the first step toward change?

2. What is an area where you feel stuck or unhappy and your energy is depleted? What do you believe is holding you back from taking action?

3. What is one step you could take toward change? What impact would taking that step have?

At this point, you should have a growing sense of what aliveness looks like and feels like for you. You've probably also pinpointed a few areas where you don't feel fully alive. You could probably list some things that you know are draining your energy and aliveness, although you might not have high hopes that they can change. Most of all, you'll see the value and urgency of making aliveness a priority in your life now rather than waiting for some distant future.

So what do you do next? How do you turn a yearning for aliveness into a reality? How do you go beyond identifying problem areas and actually fix them?

That is what we're going to discover in the following chapters. Remember the Circle of Aliveness? Each of the coming sections deals with one of the three rings within the circle. We will explore on a practical level how to adopt an Aliveness Mindset, how to have an effective Aliveness Practice, and how to identify and remain in your Optimal State.

The ultimate goal is to live in and from your OS, but I've found from experience—my own and that of leaders I've coached—that it's pretty much impossible to start with that. Why? Because there are a number of specific mindsets that are absolutely essential to even beginning this journey toward aliveness. Together, these mindsets make up what I call an Aliveness Mindset, which is the outer ring in the Circle of Aliveness.

Let's take a look at them.

PART II

ALIVENESS
MINDSET

OUR PEDALS ARE ABOUT TO START PUMPING. ARE YOU READY? HERE'S what we'll cover in part 2:

In chapter 5, we're going to look in more detail at the incredible power of the mind to shape our day-to-day experiences, and we'll see how an Aliveness Mindset—a mindset that is committed to aliveness—is an essential prerequisite to pursuing aliveness.

In chapter 6, we'll discuss the first mindset: **ownership**. This refers to accepting responsibility for your own happiness and recognizing the power and autonomy you possess to pursue it.

In chapter 7, we are going to examine the concept of **openness**, which refers to lowering your reactivity and engaging curiosity.

In chapter 8, we'll study the mindset of **awareness**. This refers to paying attention to what is in you and around you in a nonjudgmental way in order to learn more about yourself.

In chapter 9, we talk about **authenticity**. This mindset is a commitment to being truly you rather than living a life ruled by expectation, obligation, or imagined ideals.

In chapter 10, we'll cover **courage**, which is one of my favorite mindsets of all. We'll explore how courage plays into your pursuit of aliveness, especially when you need to make difficult decisions and changes.

In chapter 11, we turn our focus to **tenacity**, and we'll highlight the long-term nature of the aliveness journey and the need for grit and perseverance.

Finally, in chapter 12, we'll discuss a mindset that might seem unusual in the business world but actually has great power for creating aliveness: **love**.

IT'S ALL IN YOUR HEAD

THE OTHER DAY I WAS TALKING TO ANTHONY, A C-SUITE LEADER WHO had just come from a difficult meeting with his board chair and several others on the board. In our conversation, he went ballistic. He cursed and was frustrated that the board was critical of his work and didn't appreciate the challenges that he faced.

I couldn't help but notice how he talked about *himself*. He consistently criticized and judged himself for everything that was going wrong. Humility is a positive trait, but this wasn't humility—it was closer to self-hatred.

I could tell that working on the relational conflict with the board was going to be an uphill battle at this point, and probably unsuccessful. He was too attached to being right and blaming them. The most important issue to address wasn't the negative voices around his conference table. It was the negative voices in his head.

In our session, I began to help Anthony reframe his challenges and his role in a more self-supportive way. At one point he brought up the fact that he enjoys playing competitive basketball. We talked about the mental toughness he has as a basketball player, and we looked at how he could bring that into his approach to work issues. I watched as his mindset went from spectator to athlete, from victim to protagonist. Going forward, he had a better

perspective on himself, and that helped him make better decisions at work.

Anthony might still quit. The jury is still out on that. And
maybe he *should* quit. That's up to him. But leaving his role should
be a result of inward growth toward aliveness, not a reaction based
on frustration or fear.

A similar dynamic was at play in my own life. I felt trapped by a
job that was draining the life out of me, so I assumed my problem
was my job. But the underlying problem was less about the daily
grind of business and more about my wrong ways of thinking.

In my case, I did end up changing careers. The greatest transformation, though, was the internal one. I took ownership of my
own choices and happiness. I learned to open myself up instead of
closing myself off. I was able to accept myself as I am and be true
to that. I grew in courage and tenacity.

Those changes in my thinking, along with many others, paved
the path toward aliveness. I can't emphasize enough how grateful I
am for them. They weren't easy to learn, and I'm still growing in all
of them, but they were an entry point into my aliveness journey.

How about you? Is it possible that wrong mindsets are
hindering your experience of aliveness? Could you be harboring
ways of thinking about yourself, your job, your problems, other
people, or life in general that are draining your energy and
impeding your progress toward the best version of you?

Could you have a mindset problem?

This is a rhetorical question. We *all* have mindset problems.
There's no shame in recognizing that we've picked up some wrong
ways of thinking here and there. Nobody knows everything.
Nobody understands themselves perfectly. Nobody has the right
perspective on every situation.

A much bigger problem arises if we never identify whether our
ways of thinking are hurting us or others, or if we defend wrong

mindsets instead of learning and growing. This is why the Circle of Aliveness starts with the Aliveness Mindset. Changing how you think is the entry point into your aliveness.

So much of our success in life comes down to what's in our heads, as we'll see in a moment. That's a *good* thing. That's a freeing thing. It means we have control over it. We can change the way we think, and that will have a ripple effect on the quality of our lives.

Too often we think we are trapped by our situation when we are mostly trapped by what we are telling ourselves about our situation. We say we are blocked by obstacles when we are primarily blocked by our perspectives. We tell ourselves we are limited by our budget, by our team, by our time, or by our board of directors, when actually we are limited by our thinking.

We *must* change that.

We can change that.

Start with Your Mind

Renowned psychologist and researcher Carol Dweck has spent decades conducting groundbreaking research about how the way we think influences our leadership and lifestyle. These ways of thinking are *mindsets*, and they are remarkably powerful.[5]

A mindset refers to how your brain develops and maintains your special perspective about a particular area. It consists of your beliefs and attitudes with respect to that area. The mindsets you have adopted guide your behavior, establish your priorities, direct your decisions, and lead you to set and pursue your goals.

Dweck's research shows that our beliefs and our views of ourselves are directly tied to our future. Specifically, when we believe that our abilities and intelligence can be developed and improved, we are better able to embrace challenges, take important risks, learn from our mistakes, and persevere when things don't work out as we expected.

She famously calls this a *growth mindset*. In contrast, a *fixed mindset* is the belief that we are who we are, and we can't really change: "You can't teach an old dog new tricks." I remember one of my clients kept repeating this exact phrase as we explored the possibility of taking new actions and shifting unproductive thoughts. It was one of the shortest engagements in my practice. He couldn't adjust his perspective, and it short-circuited any attempt at growth. I believe all of us are capable of change, but some people, even though they are unhappy, are unwilling to access a growth mindset.

A growth mindset champions continuous learning over static knowing, progress over perfection, humility over ego, adaptability over rigidity. It is a way of thinking that keeps you from needing to prove yourself as a leader and instead guides you to evolve into an exponentially better, whole version of yourself.

The term *mindset* applies to more than just a growth mindset, of course, but I see a growth mindset as the OG mindset, the master of them all. If you have a growth mindset, you can change anything about how you think. But if you have a fixed mindset, you're locked into what you've always known, thought, assumed, and imagined.

Author David Robson builds on the idea of mindsets in his book *The Expectation Effect*. He writes that our brains are constantly making predictions about the future. These predictions form our expectations, which in turn have an impact on our behavior and experiences. That's why our realities are, in part, a result of our mindset. He writes, "What we feel and think will determine what we experience, which will in turn influence what we feel and what we think, in a never-ending cycle."[6] He quotes Alia Crum, an assistant professor of psychology and director of the Stanford Mind and Body Lab: "Our minds aren't passive observers, simply perceiving reality as it is. Our minds change reality. In other words, the reality we will experience tomorrow is in part a product of the mindsets we hold today."[7] I agree wholeheartedly with that statement. Since I've been a coach, I've seen over and over that our mindsets are the most powerful tools we have to impact the quality of our life.

I am living this right now in my health. The body that was so reliable during forty years of racing triathlons and marathons is nicked up. My back has issues, and for the first time ever, I have not been able to run or bike for months. I could easily feel frustrated. I could be jealous of those who are running and biking. Those things are part of me, and it feels unfair that I can't do them.

Am I going to respond to this challenge by realizing this is just a moment in time? Or am I going to let it define my perspective and dominate my emotions? Who gets to control the narrative—my circumstances or my will? The outer world or the inner me? Those are questions I often challenge my clients with when they are facing difficult moments, and I have to ask myself the same ones.

When I choose to see what I'm going through as just a moment in time, I feel gratitude. Gratitude for all of the years that I pushed my body. Gratitude for my wife, family, and fulfilling career. Gratitude for the privilege of aging, even though growing old and not being able to work out are some of my biggest fears.

What I choose to think and believe becomes my reality. I can use my mental fortitude to frame my present situation in a positive light. That, in turn, positively affects my experience of the situation. I can enjoy life even when I don't enjoy certain parts of it. I can have a positive experience even when I'm dealing with some negatives. As author James Clear writes, "At some level, every experience in life boils down to your interpretation of it. And if you can shift your mindset, then perhaps you can turn a negative experience into a positive one."[8]

Instead of focusing on not being able to run or bike, I've decided to appreciate what my body *can* do and the benefits of this new schedule. Being injured doesn't mean my life has fallen apart—it just means I have to shift my mindset and actions. Lately, I've spent more time walking. I have bumped into neighbors and friends. I have spent more time in nature. I've realized I can be just as creative walking as I could be biking. I've learned I am more resilient than I thought.

Because my mindset determines my experience, my life has not gotten worse (although I certainly miss biking!). If anything, life has only gotten better. Recently, on my sixtieth birthday, *I had the best day of my life*. I spent it with my wife and daughters. We ordered in my favorite food, and after dinner, each of them appreciated me in their own way. My heart felt open, and I felt seen and deeply connected to the most important people in my world.

That is the power of the mind. It's not junk science. It's neuroscience. It's psychology. And it's the lived experience of every one of us at one time or another.

I'm sure you've done this at some point. Maybe you were playing golf, and you hooked your drive so badly that it hit a house. Then you landed a ball in the water. Then you triple-putted. You started to get in your own head—but you stopped. You changed the mental narrative in your head. You put the past behind you and started the next hole as if nothing had happened.

Or maybe it was a challenge at work. A competitor started gaining market share. Negativity hung over the boardroom like a dark cloud. But then you and your team reframed the losses in different terms. You realized this could be the challenge you needed to become leaner, more efficient, and more creative. You got excited again, and you went into battle with a level of energy that was even greater than before.

When it comes to aliveness, we have to start with our mind. I've learned that until we address the unhealthy ways of thinking and seeing the world, it's nearly pointless to address our behaviors and emotions. Conversely, once we adopt the right mindsets, our actions, thoughts, words, feelings, decisions, and relationships fall more naturally into place.

Bottom line: keep an open mind. Don't assume old dogs can't learn new tricks. Don't assume that just because you've always believed something it must be true. As you pursue aliveness, you'll be forced to confront some of these old, rigid, fixed ways of thinking and reacting. That's not an easy thing, but it's a good thing.

Focusing your attention on your mindset helps you live intentionally rather than reactively. For example, rather than going through your day in reaction to your calendar, begin the day with a practice of deciding how you want to think and feel, such as energized, inspired, creative, and happy, regardless of what is on your calendar. Be intentional about your mindset. Stay aware of what you're thinking. Rather than being controlled from the outside in, live from the inside out.

The Aliveness Mindset

The Aliveness Mindset is made up of seven individual mindsets that frame and empower the Circle of Aliveness. These include *ownership, openness, awareness, authenticity, courage, tenacity, and love.*

This certainly isn't a comprehensive list—there are other mindsets that are important. And some of these might be more or less important to you in any given situation. Over the years as I've watched person after person grow in their level of aliveness, I've seen these seven things consistently rise to the surface.

I'm not asking you to achieve them flawlessly. Remember, this is about process, not perfection. It's about incremental, ongoing growth.

As we move through these chapters, I want you to *think about the way you think*. This is called metacognition.[9] It refers to bringing mindfulness to the ways your brain frames and regulates your attention and cognitive strategies.

This can be challenging. It can feel threatening. That's not a bad thing, but you do have to be aware of what's happening or it can freak you out. You're messing with how you act, think, and respond to life, and that's no light matter.

It works. I can't stress that enough. I've seen the results in my life and the lives of many others. When you create meaningful change in your head, it produces meaningful changes in your life.

Thinking about how you think is one of the most impactful tools you have to transform your life. It is a tool you always have access to because it exists inside of you and is completely within your control. You get to choose whether you approach life with defensiveness or eagerness, with fear or love, from reactivity or from curiosity. The mindsets you filter your world through will affect your health, happiness, and longevity, and they will shape everything you put your heart and hands to.

Let's begin by examining the mindset that opens the door to all the others: *ownership*.

1. Can you think of a time you used the power of your mind to change your outlook and behavior from negative to positive? What did you do to make that switch? What were the results?

2. Think of a few areas in your day-to-day responsibilities or behavior where you find yourself frequently complaining or unhappy with the status quo, but you feel stuck. List them below. What are some of the beliefs you are most attached to? E.g., "I have to." "That's what good leaders do." "No one else can do it as well as me."

3. How could you be more curious about those beliefs and mindsets? Would you be willing to make an argument for a new perspective about them? How could you reframe the areas that frustrate you as opportunities?

(6)

LOOK IN THE MIRROR
ALIVENESS MINDSET 1:
OWNERSHIP

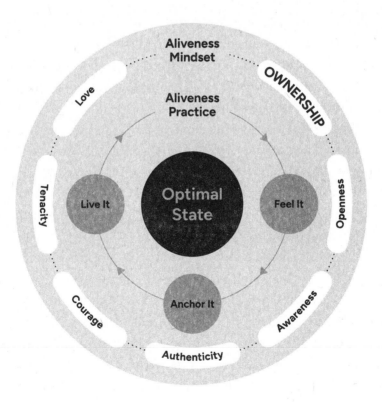

AT THE RETREAT WHERE I VENTED MY FRUSTRATION BY SCREAMING, I expected to get sympathy for my situation. I had been carrying a heavy load for a long time, and it was pretty obvious that it had taken a toll—you don't get more dramatic than screaming. So when I shared my story that weekend, I expected compassion for how hard I had labored, for how difficult my situation was at work, and for not feeling appreciated by my siblings or my family. I wanted them to pat me on the back for my good intentions.

But instead of patting me on the back, the group of leaders at the retreat smashed me in the face with feedback.

They challenged me to take responsibility for where I was at. They asked me to stop blaming others for my unhappiness. They questioned me about how I had contributed to my situation and what I could be doing differently. Taking responsibility and being accountable to yourself is ownership. I had to own that I was ultimately still responsible for my own well-being.[10]

The concept of ownership felt liberating.

If you blame other people for what you don't like about your life, you take away your power to change it. It might feel gratifying to wallow in self-pity for a while, but that's a mud pit you'll never be able to escape. At least not until you decide to take responsibility for your own aliveness.

A mindset of ownership is essential to aliveness because it gives you back your autonomy. That's why this is the first mindset we are talking about within the Aliveness Mindset. It's the key that unlocks the others. If you see yourself as nothing but a victim, if your thoughts are focused on how trapped you are by things beyond your control, you lock yourself into a cycle of "stuckness." But if you can break the cycle and realize that significant parts of your life are under your control, you move from the stifling pit of self-pity to the wide-open world of self-empowerment.

I'm not saying everything bad in your life is your fault or that it's all within your power to resolve. I'm just saying that you probably have a lot more power than you think, and your power is directly connected to your willingness to take back ownership of your life. That means being honest about what you have allowed your life to look like, why you are not making necessary changes, and what it would take to move forward.

I call this approach "Look in the Mirror" leadership, and it's an invaluable part of my coaching process. Rather than finding reasons to blame others, look in the mirror. Not to condemn yourself but to empower yourself. Own what you have done to create the current results in your life.

It wasn't easy for me to own my unhappiness, but the group that weekend helped guide me. Some of the things we identified included the following:

- I had created high, often unrealistic standards for myself and others.
- I allowed myself to resent people who could not live up to my standards.
- I expected others to know what I expected or needed even when I didn't always express it, then I resented them for not knowing how unhappy I felt.
- I chose to take on more responsibility than was asked of me.
- I chose to focus on what I didn't have instead of what I did have.
- I was living a life based on obligation.

It was an embarrassing list and a freeing one. All of that—and more—was on me. Nobody forced me to run my life and my business that way. Sure, there were factors outside my control that contributed to my work habits and mental state, such as economic pressure, business emergencies, and the normal demands of running a company. But my response to those external pressures was my responsibility, and I had to own that.

Although I felt initial resistance to the person reflected back in the mirror, I also felt a growing excitement. I previously saw my life as a prison with no options, but now I saw possibilities. Before I left that retreat, I had realized something that altered my victim mentality entirely.

No one else had to change for me to find happiness.

That truth was a powerful, liberating force. I felt an energy in my body that I hadn't sensed in my entire life. I had control. I felt alive.

A mindset of openness says, "I am ultimately responsible for the quality of my life. No one else is to blame for my dissatisfaction, and no one has to change for me to become more alive."

In psychology, the degree to which an individual believes they have control over their own life and the things that happen to them is called the "locus of control." People with an *internal* locus of control believe that outcomes they experience are a direct result of their own choices, actions, and behaviors. Those with an *external* locus of control believe that what they experience is the product of forces outside of themselves and that the circumstances they find themselves in are beyond their control.

It's important to note that you might *alternate* between these two loci, paradoxically *blend* them, or *apply them differently* to different areas of your life, such as your health, career, family, finances, and so on.[11] [12] That means that even if you are displaying ownership in one area, it doesn't mean you have mastered this mindset in every area. When you feel stuck or trapped in any area, train yourself to look inward and ask, *Have I relinquished ownership in this area?*

Always be alert to "blame creep": the sneaky, subtle, subconscious tendency to give up ownership and turn toward blame when you start to feel frustrated or trapped. How do you respond when you don't get the results you want at work? When a team doesn't reach their goals? When a leader is underperforming? When you don't feel appreciated or valued?

All of us have an "inner judger," or "inner critic" as I call it, that figures out who or what is the root cause of a problem and then looks for confirmation. If your inner judger tends to skip the self-evaluation stage and immediately jump to the finger-pointing one, you're relinquishing your role in making change without even realizing it.

When I begin working with leaders and they blame their teams, I put the spotlight back on them first. I don't ask them to blame themselves. I invite them to consider what part they have played in the result. For example, if a team member under them is under-performing, did they give clear expectations clear to that person? Did they give candid feedback on where the person stands? Did they ensure that the needed resources were available? Did they give the person a realistic time frame?

Nearly every time I ask a client this question, they are able to own what they could have done differently. I find that when they change this mindset, their thinking tends to be more productive and forward-thinking rather than focusing on the past and blaming.

There's another benefit to this approach. When a leader owns their responsibility and then gives feedback to the underperforming team member through this lens, the leader is seen more as an ally than a critic. Getting empathetic feedback from an ally leads people away from being dejected and toward better results.[13]

Interestingly, research shows that individuals with an internal locus of control demonstrate higher levels of job satisfaction than those who have an external locus of control.[14] It's probably safe to assume the same holds true for areas outside of work as well.

When we see the outcomes of our lives as largely the result of our external circumstances, we are less likely to be motivated to create change in our lives. We lose the ability to captain our own ship, because we believe that the sea is the all-powerful determinant of our direction and destiny.

This is how we lose our power—not because someone takes it from us but because we give it away.

Your aliveness is your responsibility. Can you see the freedom in that? When you own your aliveness, you give yourself permission to make the hard decisions. You probably knew you needed to make them all along, but it was easier to blame the people or problems that were frustrating or intimidating you instead of doing the hard work of change. Those things are real, but they are secondary influences on your aliveness. *You* are the primary influence. Your choices, your mental models, your emotional health, your time management, your priorities, your policies, your expectations, your inner dialogue... All of that and so much more is within your power to control. Maybe not fully, but enough to make a huge difference.

Yes, the expectations of others matter, but guess what? *You get to set those expectations.* If you let people demand everything of you, they will. Especially if you are a high-performing, skilled, intelligent leader. They'll lean on you for everything until you collapse under the weight. That doesn't make them bad people—it makes you a leader who needs to improve. They don't need you to be their messiah or their martyr. They need you to empower them and to take care of yourself so all of you can operate at your maximum potential.

Ask yourself: Does something inside you *need* to be their savior? Do you need to be needed? Are you propping up your ego at the expense of your aliveness? I know that trap well. Sometimes high-performing leaders begin to derive at least some of their sense of worth from how desperately they are needed. That's not a healthy or sustainable place to live, and it holds their team back from fulfilling their own potential.

An ownership mindset includes recognizing the unhealthy motivations behind your unhealthy practices. If you need therapy, get therapy. If you need a break, take a break. If you need to deal with insecurities, fears, attachment issues, abandonment issues, addictions, or any other internal obstacle to making healthy life choices, that's your choice and your responsibility.

I tell clients (and remind myself) of this truth all the time: *Aliveness is always within you.* It's always been there, and it always will be there, but you have to find it. You have to mine it. You have to dig it out, dust it off, turn it over in your hands, and examine it until you truly understand it.

That is the work of aliveness, and it's your work. Nobody else can do it for you.

Say it out loud: "Aliveness is within me." How do you initially react to that statement? How does it make you feel in your body and your mind? Do you believe it? Do you doubt it? Do you detect any resistance?

Relax any physical or emotional resistance and allow yourself to explore the possibility that the things you've been missing, the things you've been searching for, might be within you. Allow yourself to believe that you can find happiness even if no other person or thing around you changes. Don't try to solve the problems that pop into your mind. Just allow yourself to believe.

What feelings arise? Can you reclaim hope? Can you let excitement back in? Can you dream? Can you engage creatively with whatever you might be facing? Can you release resentment and accept responsibility?

I worked with Jonathan, a "hired gun" company president who led over a thousand employees. He had been in that role for nearly a decade, but he never felt as if the owner of the company trusted him. The owner was always guarded and standoffish in their interactions.

I asked Jonathan if he was willing to commit to making this year the best of their relationship. His energy perked up immediately. He agreed, but he told me he didn't know what he could do differently. In his mind, the owner of the company was the problem, and until his approach changed, Jonathan was stuck.

I asked him, "What would you need to do or tell yourself to make that happen?"

He replied, "I would need to feel fully trusted."

I pressed further. "What does that mean for *you*? How could you feel that way even if he doesn't change his behavior?"

He thought for a bit. "I could drop my guard and relate to him on a personal level."

I pressed further. "What is something practical you could do to make that happen?"

He said, "I can go into each meeting with an authentic smile."

We kept talking, and we brainstormed other ideas. By the time we finished, he had a handful of practical strategies to increase his own perception of trust. That didn't guarantee the owner would trust him, but that part wasn't within Jonathan's control. All he could do was work on his end of the relationship by improving his internal dialogue and assumptions. Rather than going into every interaction with suspicion or resentment, which would likely only reinforce the guarded, standoffish posture of the owner, he softened his own approach and chose to think and act as if he were trusted. And, over time, things with the owner *did* improve.

As we close this chapter, I invite you to carry that faith in yourself and your aliveness into your day. Don't wait until you finish this book or this section. Don't wait until life gets easier or your problems get smaller.

Start today. Start right now.

Aliveness is within you. It's within your reach and under your control, and that's a wildly liberating truth.

When you change your mindset from one of blame to one of ownership, a world of possibility is created. Problems that used to drain your energy now inspire greater energy. Obstacles that looked like unscalable walls become doorways to a bigger future. Frustration is no longer a place to live but simply an indicator that you still have work to do.

No, it's not always easy. But you didn't sign up for easy.

You signed up to be alive.

---

1. Think of two or three areas in your life where you are blaming someone else or feel you don't have any control. Would you be willing to take ownership for your part in the unwanted result? Take a step back and ask yourself, "What role did I play in creating this undesirable result?" (For example, "I wasn't clear on my expectations." "I didn't get buy-in." "I didn't provide enough resources.")

2. What is the value that you get out of blaming others? (For example, "The value I get is that I don't have to take responsibility."

3. What might you be avoiding? (For example, "I'm avoiding a hard conversation." "I don't want to disappoint someone.") What is the cost?

4. Can you think of a time you chose to accept ownership/responsibility for a problem that you could have blamed on other people or circumstances? How did that affect your actions going forward?

---

5. In your own words, what does "Aliveness is within me" mean?

7

ACCESSING THE ENERGY WITHIN ALIVENESS MINDSET 2: OPENNESS

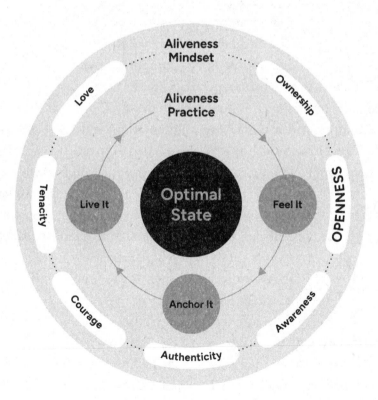

I REMEMBER ONE OF THE FIRST TIMES I TRULY EXPERIENCED ALIVENESS.

I was in Toronto, where I was leading my first team training after officially launching my coaching practice. I was nervous and excited, so naturally I had overprepared. I had created a detailed outline and an enormous online presentation deck (over one hundred slides, if I remember correctly!) that I couldn't possibly cover in the time allotted. When I tried to set up my laptop in the client's conference room, I was unable to connect to their Wi-Fi network on my laptop. I realized to my horror that I wouldn't be able to rely on the presentation deck I had worked so hard to prepare.

In the past, my natural response would have been to stress out and to believe that without the presentation deck, my training wouldn't go well. I decided to switch my thinking from fear to *openness*. I decided I wanted to be authentic, honest, and vulnerable. I chose to focus on connecting with the team, trusting I could remember whatever was important in the deck.

To my surprise, not having a presentation on the screen actually allowed me more freedom. I wasn't tied to any particular order. When I spoke about the importance of being vulnerable, I modeled vulnerability by telling them about the deck I couldn't access. We shared in the humor of the glitch, and my openness connected with them and allowed *them* to be vulnerable. As more leaders opened up, everyone's sense of psychological safety increased. It led to candid conversations about their teams and the real challenges they were facing under the surface.

I decided to lean into this idea of openness and honesty even more. I began giving examples of when I'd faced challenges similar to the ones I knew they might be facing. I talked about mistakes I had made as a CEO of my business. I shared the times where I didn't have everything figured out and didn't know the answer. I thought of times when I became reactive and wasn't my best as a leader. I shared times that I avoided asking my team for help because I thought that it would make me look bad.

None of those things were in my presentation, but they turned out to be the key to creating an incredibly honest, healthy environment. People quickly opened up and became vulnerable. We began to challenge our belief that leaders should have all of the answers and not ask for help because "that's what good leaders do." Because of the level of trust and connection we had built, everyone seemed more open to accepting responsibility for unwanted results instead of blaming others. Things felt less serious. We laughed a lot as we looked in the mirror at our unproductive patterns.

Not only did my openness create trust with the team, it transformed the way I led the sessions. I felt present, confident, and connected. My body was relaxed and authentic. I trusted my intuition. I intuitively used skills I had learned in the past as a litigator and amateur stand-up comic to engage the team of twenty leaders. I surprised myself with my creativity, command of the room, and ability to improvise. I felt tingly, electric bursts of energy in my body, which I later came to recognize as part of my aliveness experience.

That experience showed me just how important and effective a *mindset of openness* is. Because I chose to respond to a challenge with vulnerability, honesty, and curiosity, I was able to adapt and pivot, which made the experience better, not worse. Even more importantly, my openness was contagious. It fostered an atmosphere of vulnerability and authenticity. We engaged in powerful, candid, effective conversations.

In order to be truly open I had to overcome my natural tendency toward reactivity. The same held true for those twenty leaders. They had to move past the reactivity, defensiveness, and self-protective tendencies that are so natural to all of us before they could imagine a better way of leading.

Research indicates that an open mind coupled with humility facilitates learning, adaptation to diverse environments, and innovation.[15] The longer I coach, the more convinced I am that reactivity is one of the greatest enemies leaders face, and openness is the antidote. As a matter of fact, I don't believe you can experience ongoing aliveness without learning how to get out of a reactive state and into an open one. One of the better models to increase your awareness of being open or reactive is found in Julia Galef's book *The Scout Mindset*. Scouts seek to understand first. They model openness. Soldiers, on the other hand, defend a position and are reactive.[16] Reactivity often happens when we are attached to being right about an issue or situation.

The way I am using it in this book, *reactivity is an automatic, triggered response to a perceived threat*. Reactivity occurs when we have a spontaneous response to what is occurring in and around us. We believe that in some way our approval, security, or control are in jeopardy. We seek these core human needs to feel safe. Often, this reactivity is more than just a momentary response: it's a state of mind. It's a habit and lifestyle of leadership that we come to assume is normal. We call it "work pressure" or "the demands of the job," but in reality it's a mindset of reactivity.

Why is openness the antidote to reactivity? Because reactivity is an automatic reaction, which means you do it without thinking about it. Being open, on the other hand, engages intentionality and reflexivity. When you focus on being open, you are able to understand why you are reacting in a particular way, what you feel threatened by, and whether that threat is real or not. Reactivity is like a ticking bomb, and openness is the tool to defuse it.

I was working with a CEO named Denise whose company had recently acquired another home goods retail chain. Besides coaching Denise one-on-one, I was also working with the executive teams of both her current company and the acquired company to help facilitate a healthy acquisition. The leaders of the acquired company shared with me that they did not feel appreciated for their expertise and were not involved in setting goals, yet they were responsible to reach the goals set by Denise. When they tried to have a direct conversation with her, Denise was dismissive and angry.

When I talked with Denise at our next session, she acknowledged that she was under stress and overwhelmed. She said she had underestimated the complexity of transitioning the new team into a productive role. I suggested that she think of examples when she was most open to feedback. I encouraged her to assume positive intent: to believe that the newly acquired team wanted to help the company grow. Her reactivity instantly diminished. She began to envision the combined teams being successful and collaborating.

Denise then reached out to the leaders from the acquired team and was more open and available to actively listen to them. She expressed that she should have done a better job communicating strategy and the reasoning behind the goals, and she should have solicited their input on what goals were realistic. The team from the acquired company felt more heard and had several good suggestions about how to improve the growth strategy.

I could give dozens of other examples of leaders and teams I've worked with that have had to learn to defuse their reactivity by choosing openness. This is one of the first things I talk about with clients because I find that many high-functioning leaders live in a state of continual reactivity. When it comes to leading their businesses and their teams, they are not paying attention to their own aliveness. Typically they are more focused on outcomes. Are we meeting our sales goals? Are we meeting our production mark? Are we generating enough of a profit for our investors? Can we do everything faster? They are reacting to data and demands.

They are putting out fires. This is how the business world typically functions, but it leads to exhaustion, burnout, stress, and anxiety. Decisions and actions come from a place of fear and scarcity rather than a place of intentionality and open-mindedness.

One of my clients described the difference between reactivity and openness this way: he said it's like going from being on your *heels* of your feet to being on the *balls* of your feet. Being on your heels is defensive. It's reactionary. It's about control. Being on the balls of your feet is proactive, exploratory, on the move. It's about curiosity.

I've had a few years to reflect on my experience running a company, and I realize that to a high degree, my jam-packed schedule, my tendency to overcommit and overwork, my perfectionism, and the unrealistic expectations I had of myself were due to a reactive mindset. I had a JD (juris doctor) from Kent College of Law, but I had a PhD in reactivity and fear. I would go into action, accomplish something, check off a box, and let the adrenaline from that carry me on to the next task. I didn't leave myself room to feel my anxiety long enough to learn from it or to release it from my system. It just stayed there, hidden below the surface, undermining my aliveness because I didn't handle it correctly. The pattern I see in myself, and the one I see in so many of the leaders I work with, is that from the moment we wake up in the morning, our focus is running away from fear and mitigating risk and loss rather than running toward our full potential.

It's interesting to me that reactivity has nothing to do with how much money my clients have made or how much success they've had. So many of them still struggle with imposter syndrome. They still have worries about money. They face the same inner challenges and hear the same anxiety-inducing voices as anyone else.

We all experience fear, worry, anxiety, and stress. But we also all have the opportunity to live above those things. To defuse reactivity by embracing openness. To replace control with curiosity. To shift our mental posture from the heels of our feet to the balls of our feet.

In a world filled with reasons to be stressed out and overwhelmed, how do we move from reactivity to openness? One of the best ways is to *pay attention* to those things. To listen to them, learn from them, and choose how to respond to them.

This might seem counterintuitive. Generally, we aren't taught to value "negative" emotions such as fear and anxiety. They are things to fix, deny, avoid, or push through until we can finally be free and happy. That's impossible. If we're waiting until we have nothing to fear before we feel alive, it will never happen. Even worse, if we allow ourselves to live in reactivity, we'll actually undermine our own aliveness. We'll move away from our best self, not toward it.

That's where openness comes in.

Let me explain. Earlier I defined reactivity as an automatic, triggered response to a perceived threat. Think about the word *threat*. A threat can be specific and immediate, such as when a business deal is about to fall through or a lawsuit is pending, or it can be more general and long-term, such as the underlying concern you might carry about company profits or growing competition.

Interestingly, neuroscience distinguishes between the *fear* that is triggered by immediate threats and the *anxiety* that is created by long-term, generalized threats. This differentiation between fear and anxiety can be attributed to the work of renowned neuroscientist Joseph LeDoux.[17] LeDoux showed that the brain actually processes these kinds of threats differently.

Most of us deal with both fear and anxiety regularly because we face both short-term and long-term threats. That means that when it comes to reactivity, either fear or anxiety (or a combination of the two) can be the source. For example, when

unexpected bad news comes, your brain can instantly jump
into reactivity because the threat is real, present, and scary
(*fear*). But you can also *live* in reactivity if you are constantly
carrying the weight of long-term concerns in an unhealthy way
(*anxiety*). It might be low-level reactivity, but it's still there, and
it's stealing your aliveness.

Often we think we can get out of our reactive state by solving
the short-term threats that trigger us, but that's flawed reasoning.
First, you'll never solve them all because more will come along to
take their place. Second, solving immediate threats doesn't address
the long-term threats that create a lifestyle of anxiety.

So what do these things have to do with openness? Everything.
Threats of any kind tend to trigger unconscious fight-or-flight
reactions. They shut you down. They close you off. They make you
defensive and reactive.

Openness, on the other hand, is a decision to engage the
rational part of your brain. You move from unconscious reaction
to conscious action. By listening and learning to the things that
cause fear or anxiety, you disable the automatic fight-or-flight
response and replace it with curiosity. Then, you learn more about
yourself and what you really value, want, and need. You see what
is getting in the way of those things.

Anxiety, in particular, can be an indication that something
inside of you is out of alignment. This can be difficult to identify
because when you feel anxiety or stressed, you probably tend to
look for an outside stimulus to blame. Often it's your body's way of
telling you that you are not in a healthy mental or emotional place.

In these instances, fear and anxiety can show you exactly how
you are limiting yourself. They can reveal how you are interfering
with your own aliveness. Instead of ignoring or suppressing this
incredible built-in tool, work *with* fear and anxiety by engaging
openness. How do you do that?

Step 1: Don't ignore it; listen to it.

What if, instead of ignoring fear, you listened to it? What if, instead of denying anxiety, you asked it questions? This is about awareness. About self-knowledge. About honesty and maturity. The next time you feel afraid or worried, ask yourself, *What does this emotion reveal about me? About my motivations? About my insecurities? About my value system? About my priorities? About my assumptions? About my mental models? How can I know myself better through what I'm feeling?* Remove the guilt or shame associated with fear and anxiety and replace it with curiosity and openness.

Step 2: Don't kill it; tame it.

While you cannot eradicate fear or anxiety, you don't have to let them control you either. Your thoughts and emotions are your responsibility, and outside circumstances don't have the right to control them. So when you feel afraid or worried, don't fight it—but don't give in to it either. Don't let your mind get carried away with infinite catastrophes and worst-case scenarios. Take ownership of your thoughts and "tame the lion" rather than vanquishing it altogether.

Step 3: Don't let it use you; use it instead.

Use fear and anxiety as the warning systems they are designed to be. Let them inform you when you are off track, when you are focused on what you don't have or on losing what you do have. Use them as a signal to move out of reactivity into openness. Turn your attention deeper, toward the power within you, tapping into moments where you feel at your best. Then take that feeling and make it your baseline instead of fear and anxiety.

I'm not saying that all fears are healthy or that all anxiety is your friend, but I believe that every emotion and feeling can teach you something, even the "negative" ones. You won't know that until you open yourself up—until you defuse the subconscious, automatic reactivity that keeps you back on your heels by choosing a mindset of openness. When you become open, vulnerable, and curious, fear loses its power to control you, and it becomes simply one more teacher that is leading you toward self-awareness and aliveness.

A mindset of openness not only defuses reactivity but also becomes a continual source of new energy. By energy, I am referring to the intangible, inner life force that motivates you, inspires you, and sustains you. The concept of "energy" was one I didn't have words for when I was a leader. At the time, I thought my frustration and anxiety were a result of outward pressures. In reality, they were indicators that I was not truly alive, because aliveness and energy go hand in hand.

The amount and kind of energy we feel is directly connected to our aliveness. Nonliving things have a nonsustainable relationship to energy. A bonfire, for example, will let off a great deal of energy, but at some point it will burn out. The sun will eventually go dark. A car can go only as far and as fast as its fuel supply will allow it. In other words, nonliving things consume energy, but they don't have the capacity to create, maintain, and depend on an energy cycle the way that living things do.

Living things constantly and autonomously open themselves to receive energy from the world around them and convert it into something they can use to thrive. Living things receive energy and use energy. They create it and they consume it. It's a continuous cycle that relies on openness, transformation, and release. Michael Singer, in his book *Untethered Soul*, refers to this as "infinite energy."[18]

If your energy is running out, if you're getting burned out rather than finding yourself continually renewed, it could be a sign that you need to check your level of aliveness. It's likely that you have moved from a state of openness to one of reactivity, because reactivity is about protecting, hoarding, and controlling, and that ultimately will block your experience of aliveness.

Michael Singer emphasizes the need to feed energy through staying open. He writes,

> The more you stay open, the more energy flow can build. At some point, so much energy comes into you that it starts flowing out of you. You feel it as waves pouring off of you. You can actually feel it flowing off of your hands, out of your heart, and through other energy centers. All these energy centers open, and a tremendous amount of energy starts flowing out of you. What is more, the energy affects other people. People can pick up on your energy, and you're feeding them with this flow. If you are willing to open even more, it never stops. You become a source of light for all those around you.[19]

What does openness look like for you? I can't tell you that. At least not in detail. It's something you have to discover for yourself. The same holds true for reactivity. You have to pay attention to your reactions, your responses, your internal dialogue, and even the way people respond to you in order to learn how reactivity and openness manifest in your life.

As you do, you'll get better and better at quickly identifying reactivity and moving to openness. It will become almost second nature to you, one of those quick self-correction things you do, like when you catch yourself slouching and remind yourself to stand up straight, or when you're clenching your teeth and you tell yourself to relax your jaw. You'll get better at noticing when you're closed and defensive. You'll get better at opening your mind and heart. You'll learn to be curious instead of controlling, authentic instead of authoritarian.

Do you need more energy? Openness can help create that flow for you.

Do you find yourself reacting in ways you don't like? Openness can give you the knowledge you need to choose healthy reactions.

Do voices of fear have more control over your attitude than you'd like? Openness will help restore your peace and balance your emotions.

The choice is yours. You can't control the outside world, but you can open up your inner world. And when you do, your life will change. Your leadership will too. Once you get a taste of the freedom and energy that openness brings, and once you recognize how small and constrained a life of reactivity is, you'll become passionate about remaining in a state of openness as much as possible.

1. What is one thing you could do today to be more open, curious, and less reactive?

2. What does reactivity look like in your life and leadership? Can you give a recent example of a time you were reactive and what emotions (sadness, anger, or fear) you felt? Did you feel a threat to a core human need (approval, control, or security)?

3. If you were with others when this occurred, how did they react to your behavior? What did you leave in your wake? Were they left feeling depleted or energized? Defeated or inspired? Confused or clear?

4. In general, when is it hard for you to be open? When have others told you that they did not feel heard? Think of a few specific examples. In those situations, what were you closed to, or what were you certain you were right about? If you were to be more open, what questions should you have asked? What beliefs would you have to change?

8

THE FIRST STEP
TO (ANY) CHANGE
ALIVENESS MINDSET 3:
AWARENESS

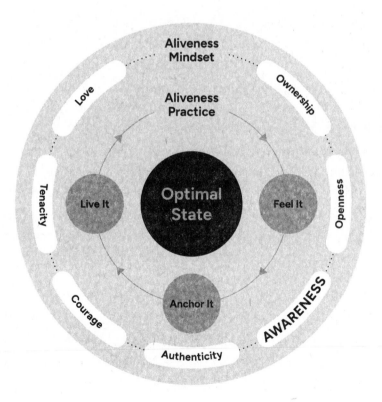

ONCE YOU HAVE TAKEN *OWNERSHIP* OF YOUR ALIVENESS AND ADOPTED a mindset of *openness* rather than reactivity, the next step is to learn to practice *awareness*. Specifically, I'm talking about awareness of your level of aliveness in any given moment.

More than anything, this takes intentionality. Once you decide to analyze what you are thinking or feeling, you can often identify problem areas within a matter of seconds. What are you feeling? What are you afraid of? What is triggering you? What could you do to recover your aliveness?

The questions almost answer themselves. But they don't *ask* themselves. You have to do that. You have to stop and think about it.

I recently worked with a sales leader named Julie. She worked at a software as a service (SaaS) company that was navigating an economic downturn and had to reduce headcount and pivot strategically. During this complex, delicate process, she bounced ideas around with several trusted leaders on her team about how they were going to adapt to the challenges.

At one point, several other leaders on her team shared that they didn't feel valued or involved in key strategy decisions. Julie immediately snapped at them. She said that they had to trust her and that it would slow the process to consult with everyone. Julie ruminated for the rest of the day about the leaders' feedback and hurt feelings. She knew her reaction was not helpful, but she felt powerless to move past her reactive state.

When we met, I asked her to take a few deep breaths and notice any tension in her body. I reminded her that we tend to resist negative emotions, and often we are not even aware of how tension feels in our bodies. I encouraged her to focus on the sensations in her body and asked her if she could allow the sensation to be there.

Then I said, "What emotions do you have?"

The first thing she said was, "Anger! I can't ask everyone to be involved in every decision." She began to express her thoughts and judgments, and I could see it was actually making her reactive again.

I encouraged her to stay in her body: to be aware of what she was feeling rather than to be carried away by it. I asked her if she would be willing to try to reduce the duration and intensity of her reactivity. She agreed, of course. Most of us don't *want* to be reactive. It's a state we find ourselves in without trying to go there, and it takes awareness and intentionality to get out of it.

Then I asked, "Are you experiencing any other emotions?"

She thought for a second, then replied, "Fear. I'm scared that I don't know how to lead this complex and talented team and that I'm losing their confidence."

I pressed further. "Do you feel any other emotions?"

I saw a flash of realization. "I'm sad," she said. "I respect my team and they work so hard. I feel terrible that they don't feel included."

I could see her body relax. Recognizing the emotions that were hiding under her anger released some of the pressure Julie was feeling. She was now more open to hearing their experience of feeling left out of the decision process. That subtle shift helped her tap into her empathy and created more space for her to reflect on the situation.

We kept talking. I asked her, "Are any of your core needs feeling threatened?" As humans, the more our core needs (approval, control, and security) are threatened, the more we tend to get reactive.[20] [21]

She had to think about that one for a second. "The approval of my team," she replied. We explored that thought for a little bit. Julie acknowledged that she wanted to know where people stand on issues. She knew it took courage for them to express that they felt left out. Although she felt like the approval of her team was being threatened, if anything, they were showing trust in her and faith in the shared mission by going to her with their complaints. Rather than getting defensive or feeling hurt by their comments, Julie realized the input was a sign of a healthy team.

Then we started talking about aliveness and her Optimal State. In a previous session, we had identified her OS. We'll talk more about discovering your OS in a later chapter, but if you remember our definitions at the beginning of the book, your OS is your personal experience of aliveness. It's the state of being where you feel most alive and where you consistently bring the best version of yourself into your day-to-day experience.

I asked her to say her Optimal State aloud, and she said, "Inspirational." The second she said it, we both laughed. She said, "My initial reaction to my team doesn't seem very inspirational, does it?" I asked if there was one thing she could do to return to her OS.

She closed her eyes and paused. "We could meet and discuss how I can get their input. I could thank them for their feedback and acknowledge that I could see how they felt left out."

I asked, "Is that what an inspirational leader would do?"

Julie replied, "That is exactly what an inspirational leader would do." She had left her reactive state and was reclaiming her aliveness. And it all happened because she was willing to become more aware.

No matter what circumstances we are facing, we have the capacity to control our actions like Julie did. This tool is always within reach and easy to use. Plus, the more we engage in mindset shifts in moments of reactivity, the easier it becomes. We develop an awareness mindset, an awareness habit, that allows us to internally reflect regularly and course correct as needed.

I'm calling awareness a mindset because, just as with the other mindsets, it's a mental model that you choose to engage. I'm not talking about a one-time "aha!" moment but about a lifestyle of looking inward. It's about deciding to pay attention to *you*, which is something high-performing leaders are not always good at. My clients can usually rattle off their company's valuation, last-quarter earnings, and projected next-quarter profits, but they often struggle to put words to their deepest wants, fears, and dreams.

Notice that with Julie, the questions I asked weren't particularly profound. The point isn't the questions: it's the inward gaze. It's the decision to stop, even for a few minutes, and focus on what you're feeling.

Your day should begin with an awareness of you at your best, of how you want to feel throughout your day, and of what you need to do to create that experience for yourself. That means taking a few moments every morning and as needed throughout the day to intentionally engage with an aliveness mentality.

Ask yourself, *What activities will enhance aliveness and which ones will lower my energy? Am I aware of my limits? My triggers? My values? My body? My feelings? My fears? My patterns? My genius?*

Awareness is the starting point for all change. If your car is making funny noises, you can't fix it until you figure out what's wrong. If your back has been bothering you for months, you probably won't improve until you discover what is out of whack. It's common sense. In the same way, if you aren't consistently experiencing aliveness, you need to stop and ask yourself what's wrong or nothing will ever change.

That sounds so easy, but life moves at such a fast pace that we rarely do it. Plus, many of us were never taught to stop, to reflect, to ask. Instead, we were taught to do, to go, to build, to conquer, to produce.

That's why many of us have sacrificed our authentic selves for productivity. It's why we've been held captive by our calendar and to-do list for years. *We unconsciously function from expectation rather than inspiration.* We let what is on our agenda impact our mood rather than letting our energy drive our agenda and our contribution to the world. We have been indoctrinated into the mindset of doing first rather than being first.

Nobody encouraged us to slow down. There's no time for slowing down in business, right? While you're sitting cross-legged on a yoga mat taking deep breaths and connecting with your inner child, your competition is running an ad campaign to steal market share. Or at least that's what we've been told.

Or maybe that's what we tell ourselves. Why? Because we're secretly afraid of what awareness might reveal. It's scary to sit with our feelings. It's scary to ask if we are happy. It's scary to evaluate if this is what we want to do and who we want to be.

That's where I was stuck for years. It was easier to stuff my feelings deep inside and tell myself I'd deal with them later. ("I'm great at compartmentalizing," says every leader who fails to understand that this is a myth.) It was easier to stay so busy that I never had to address those existential moments where I wondered if this was really all there was to life. It wasn't really easier, because it was killing me. But it felt easier in the moment.

Once I began to gain awareness of who I was, what I valued, and how my work environment was affecting my inner world, I gained so much clarity. That clarity led to courage, and eventually I was able to reshape my life in a way that amplified my aliveness rather than undermining it.

Most of the time, awareness as a mindset and a tool doesn't lead to massive changes like closing your company or changing your career. They don't need to because if you're truly aware, you'll make small changes along the way. Julie was a great example:

her awareness allowed her to make corrections in real time that brought her back around to her own version and experience of aliveness.

Let me give you another example. Steve, the founder and CEO of a billion-dollar B2B tech company, often felt overwhelmed and at the mercy of his calendar. Correction: he had *allowed* himself to be at the mercy of his calendar. His team invited him to meeting after meeting, filling up day after day. Steve felt obligated to attend those meetings because he didn't want to let his team down or he didn't trust that the team would take action the way he wanted. His day started at 8:00 a.m., and meetings filled his calendar until 6:00 p.m. At night, exhausted and drained, he would begin what felt like his "real work."

Steve complained to me that he felt depleted and that his team took too much of his time. Yet he was resistant to saying no, setting boundaries, or having honest conversations about under-performing leaders. He equated rejecting meeting invites with not supporting his team, and he believed that he didn't have time to replace underperforming leaders. He let those beliefs drive his decisions regarding his calendar.

I often challenge my clients to attend meetings only where their value add is $10,000/hour. That's not an exact amount: it's actually a strategy to get them to think about why they are in these meetings and what value they're adding. This is an awareness issue. Are they attending out of habit? Because it makes them feel important? Because they need control? Because they don't trust their team? Because they don't want to disappoint anyone? Putting a dollar amount on their time forces them to be intentional about their priorities, and that brings awareness to their motivations.

What Steve could not see was that his beliefs locked him into an unhealthy cycle and sapped his aliveness. His definition of aliveness was "connection," yet he couldn't think of many moments in his week when he felt connected to his team. In fact, he felt very disconnected.

Nothing could change until Steve became aware of what was happening. He needed to see that saying yes to his team all the time actually equated to a lack of support for himself, and that was bad for both his company and his employees. He had to gain awareness not only of the negative emotions he was feeling but also the toll they were taking on him and the underlying mindsets that were undermining his efforts to feel differently. Then, he had to become aware of how he wanted to feel. He had to discover what mindsets and habits would create that feeling of aliveness.

When I worked with him to see the flipside of his frustration— that is, to identify the things that supported his aliveness, rather than detracting from it—he reoriented his own thinking and lifestyle.

First, he practiced awareness regarding his energy for the meetings on his calendar for the coming week. For those where his energy was lowest, he broke them into two categories: He told some of the teams that he was going to experiment with no longer attending; instead, he asked for a summary of what happened and also gave them feedback on what would improve those meetings. For the remaining meetings on his calendar where his energy was low, he asked those teams to make the case that his attendance was worth $10,000/hour. In half of those meetings, the leaders were unable to provide a strong enough justification for him to attend, so he eventually stopped going to those as well.

These changes had a dramatic effect on Steve's energy. He could feel his aliveness meter rising, and that motivated him to become even more aware of what was working against aliveness and what was working toward it.

He decided he needed to face conversations that he was avoiding. This was another moment of awareness. He already knew that underperforming leaders were a drain—that was obvious because it affected the team's success. But he realized his own hesitancy to have difficult conversations meant he lived with a constant burden of guilt and anxiety.

He scheduled overdue conversations with leaders who were underperforming and gave them clear timelines and expectations for their improvement. He let go of one of the leaders in question within three months.

Over the next six months, Steve focused on his feeling of aliveness daily, and he was intentional about how and where he spent his time. He got energized when he saw the positive impact he was having on his team with his newfound time and energy. He was able to focus on the company's growth strategy, and the company's sales forecast was revised upward as a result.

As you can see from Steve's example, actions are what produce change, but awareness is what shows you what actions to take. Too often we try to make changes out of frustration, fear, or anger, but we just make the problem worse because we are acting from ignorance, not awareness.

Take time to become aware. Take time to truly see and understand. Be aware of the situation at hand, but even more importantly, be aware of you. Remember, awareness is more than just self-improvement. It's one thing to try to constantly improve, but it's another to sit with your feelings, thoughts, hopes, fears, and dreams until you gain a more complete understanding of your situation.

Remember also that awareness includes both the negative and the positive feelings you have. Actually it's hard to separate the two because even the "negative" things you feel can help you become more alive. They are there to point you away from what is hurting you and toward what is helping you.

How does your life feel right now? Do you feel hope, energy, and aliveness? Or do you feel like screaming into the void, or into someone's face? For me, it took a weekend away and a group of supportive peer leaders to help me be honest with myself. It doesn't have to be that way. If you embrace awareness as a daily practice, you'll grow in your ability to understand yourself and make changes as needed.

There are no right or wrong answers. The goal is to be honest with where you are so you can evaluate where you want to go. Don't tell yourself what you "should" feel. Don't force yourself to feel the "right" emotions or the "good" feelings. Don't align your emotional state to what others want you to feel or need you to feel. Don't be quick to label what you feel as good or bad. Don't rush through the uncomfortable feelings, either, or deny them, ignore them, or push them aside.

Just feel.

Look directly at what is happening in your mind and heart. Become aware of who you are, what you need, what works for you, what you are good at, what you are bad at, and what is creating the life you are meant to have.

Only then will you be able to make informed, wise choices that lead you toward greater aliveness.

1. Once again, think of a time when you became very reactive. What was your thought or judgment?
   What did you do or say next? Did you take action and act impulsively? How did others impact your actions?

2. Think of a time when you were reactive but you slowed down, paused, and evaluated yourself. What were your emotions? What were your biggest fears or concerns? What helped you slow down or gain perspective? What was the result?

3. Here are two ways to increase your awareness of your weaknesses and your blind spots:
   a) Ask people who work for you, or are close to you, to give you feedback in the moment when you are reactive. Have them describe what they are observing. Thank them for giving you the feedback. Avoid explaining, rationalizing, or justifying your behavior.
   b) When you are reactive, are you able to notice all of your emotions (sadness, anger, fear)? Do you notice your thoughts? Do you notice what it feels like in your body?

4. Take two minutes right now and be still. Set a timer so you don't have to check the time. What are you feeling about your business, family, and personal life? How would you rate these areas on a scale of 1–10? For each category, what do you need to do to make it a 10? If you can't think of an answer now, reflect on these questions for the next few days.

9

THE BEST YOU IS THE REAL YOU ALIVENESS MINDSET 4: AUTHENTICITY

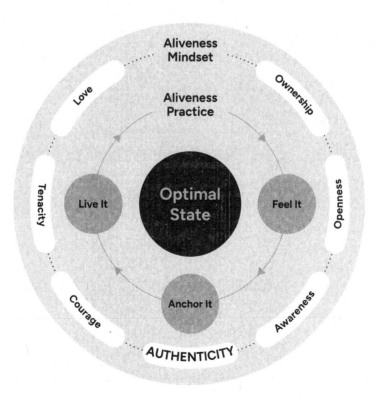

As I SHARED EARLIER, FOR OVER TWENTY YEARS, I ASSUMED THE roles of being the best father, husband, son, and leader I could. I expected perfection from myself and held myself to the highest standards. Over time, I became exhausted. I was no longer aware of the real me: the part of me that no longer wanted to run the business, that was scared, that didn't have all the answers, that didn't always feel appreciated, that blamed others, that got angry and had a hard time asking for what I really wanted.

In hindsight, I think a lot of my own unhappiness was rooted in trying to be someone I was not. I was missing *authenticity*. I find a lot of my clients have similar challenges when it comes to being authentic.

I began by letting out my authenticity in small doses. I started with sharing more of my thoughts and feelings with others. I kept identifying layers that masked the real me, and I worked on removing them. For the most part, these parts of me were accepted and appreciated by others. Part of my work was that I accepted those parts of me that didn't live up to my exacting standards. I asked for what I wanted and was surprised by the number of times I heard "yes."

What was most surprising was that others could sense my sincerity and authenticity. They were drawn to my ability to be vulnerable and allow others to judge me or appreciate me. I (mostly) let go of managing my image and what others thought. I began to feel lighter. I felt more connected to others. I became less serious, and I incorporated more play into my day-to-day experiences.

Then I took action by pursuing the idea of becoming a coach. The more that I identified my true wants, the more energy I felt. I realized that my potential and dreams were far greater than I imagined when I was inauthentic. I created a company and a job that was fulfilling, impactful, fun, and provided me with a dream lifestyle of flexibility and income.

When I was running my business, I rarely, if ever, felt alive. This version of me feels alive almost every single day.

Authenticity refers to the degree to which your life aligns with your true self rather than conforming to societal expectations or external pressures. Author Brené Brown defines it as "the daily practice of letting go of who we think we are supposed to be and embracing who we are."[22] It involves being true to *your* values, desires, and beliefs, instead of playing a role.

Why would you play a role? Maybe because it's what is expected of you. Maybe out of obligation. Maybe because you are "being responsible." Maybe to reach a financial or career goal. Maybe to fit in and gain acceptance. Maybe to keep control. Maybe out of fear of losing what you have. Whatever the reason or reasons, you find yourself living and leading in a way that isn't completely true to the real you.

In his book *The Power of Regret*, Daniel Pink references the work of psychologist Tory Higgins from the 1980s. Higgins proposed that individuals hold three self-perceptions: the *actual* self (how they currently see themselves to be), the *ideal* self (how they aspire to be), and the *ought* self (how they believe they should be). Higgins emphasized that when these self-perceptions are not in harmony, it can lead to discomfort and distress. For example, when the actual self doesn't align with the ideal self, it can result in emotions like sadness and dissatisfaction. If the actual self doesn't match the ought self, it can trigger emotions like fear and restlessness.[23]

Daniel Pink argues that the gap between our actual self and our ought or ideal selves is what fuels much of our regret.[24] In my coaching practice, I've spoken with many business leaders who are experiencing frustration with this gap, just as I was feeling years ago. Their life seems good on the surface, but it is not bringing true aliveness on the inside. They are recognizing, often after years of hard work and dedicated service, that they've settled for a life that's less than optimal instead of growing into the aliveness they are capable of experiencing. Rather than giving up or living with regret, they're ready to level up.

How about you? Have you tolerated or settled for a not-so-bad existence in the name of duty, habit, or gratitude? If so, own it. Acknowledge it. Accept it. It's a strange dichotomy: you can be grateful and discontent at the same time. You can recognize your blessings, your privileges, and the gifts life has given to you, while also recognizing that you haven't been fully honest with yourself about certain areas of dissatisfaction.

Remember also that a key component of authenticity is self-acceptance. It's about being okay with the real you. It means you don't carry an obligation to be who others want you to be or even who you think you should be. You are not always the best boss or parent. You will disappoint people at times. You are not like anyone else. Don't excuse things that need to change, but don't hate or hide who you really are either.

I encourage my clients to take a breath of self-compassion when they are bringing out more of their authentic self. I invite them to think, *This is the real me. This is the real me who may not be available every time my spouse or partner needs me. This is the real me who disappoints people at times. This is the real me who sometimes needs a break when there's a responsibility and it's my turn.*

After they have shared their authentic selves, I ask, "Can you accept this part of yourself? Can you be okay if others are disappointed or angry?"

Often the answer to those last questions is "no" or, "I'm having a hard time." Bringing out your authentic self is a process of layers. It's worth it because the cost of not being authentic can be burnout, resentment, and disconnection.

After self-acceptance, authénticity moves to alignment. How can you live, work, love, grow, and play in a way that aligns with who you really are? This is the heart of an authenticity mindset.

Think about the areas where you feel you have to adapt or not be your true self. Then ask yourself this question: Is there something I could do right now to be truer to myself? That simple question will open your mind to a world of possibility. You don't have to change everything, but can you change one thing? When you make that question a litmus test for your day-to-day choices, you'll begin to experience the power of an authenticity mindset.

For example, at the end of the last chapter, you rated your business, family, and personal life on a scale of 1–10, then jotted down ideas to improve that score. Look back at your answers and notice how they naturally flow from authenticity. That is, notice how the action steps you identified flow from what you authentically desire for that area of your life.

When you choose to be true to yourself, you are forced to confront the areas where you have settled for less. I don't mean you spiral into discontentment or that you play the victim. I mean you become honest with where *you* have made the choice to compromise your true self for some sort of gain. Remember your aliveness journey begins with ownership, openness, and awareness: you can't come to a place of absolute honesty until you take responsibility for yourself and make conscious choices to explore who you are.

One of the best ways to identify areas where you are inauthentic is to examine what you want or wish for. That sounds so selfish, doesn't it? And that's the problem. We think our wants are superficial and selfish rather than realizing that often they are just trying to alert us to ways we have settled for something that isn't aligned with who we truly are. What you want is often the key to discovering what you need.

I remember a funny moment—and a very revealing one—from that first CLG retreat that helped me understand this. Toward the end, we were asked to think of things that we wanted and hadn't expressed. It was a very challenging exercise for me. One of my core beliefs, modeled by my father, was that a good husband, father, and business owner should take care of the needs of his wife, kids, and business first. That meant that stating my own wants and needs translated to selfishness.

One by one, everyone stood up and identified their desires: a better job, a loving life partner, a healthier lifestyle. After each person spoke, the group applauded. Then it was my turn. I literally could not name something I wanted because I was so conditioned to putting aside my own desires.

Finally, a want popped in my mind, and I blurted, "I want a banana every day with my breakfast!"

The room erupted with laughter. Someone said, "*That's* your want? A banana?"

I explained that it was hard for me to ask for support or to ask for what I wanted. I ate yogurt every day with fruit, and a fresh, ripe banana was the key component. I wanted my wife to support me by ensuring that we always had bananas available for breakfast.

They got a good laugh out of it. But it was a breakthrough for me. I realized I didn't have to justify every want. I could just *want* something. Period. That is part of being human, and there's nothing wrong with it.

Prior to that moment, I always judged my wants. They were too selfish, too silly, too shallow. I had confused emotional martyrdom and denying my own needs with being a hard worker, a good provider, and a successful businessman. The banana was a little bit of a breakthrough, and it set me on a path toward ever-greater authenticity.

That's a path you must take too. If you're going to experience true aliveness, you can't shut off sections of your soul. You can't live a life defined by other people's demands or by an idealized version of what you "should" do. Inauthenticity and aliveness don't play well together.

I believe that regularly tuning into your wants is a skill that must be developed, and it is one that leads to bigger and bolder wants. What do you want? What want would get you excited, bring a smile to your face, and help you feel more alive? What do you really need to experience in business, in relationships, in finances, in health, in your emotions? You don't have to justify that. You don't have to earn it. You don't have to get permission from someone else to have it.

Obviously I'm not talking about being an asshole. Most clients I work with don't struggle with being an asshole. They struggle with honesty. They struggle with recognizing and pursuing what they need and want out of life. They are hard workers who are used to doing whatever it takes to keep their business afloat, who know what it's like to sit at the desk where the buck always stops, who have grown used to being human shock absorbers who take the hits so their team doesn't feel the full impact.

That takes a toll after a while. And if you don't learn to be honest, if you don't have the conversations and make the adjustments you need to along the way, bad things happen. You burn out. You give up. You have panic attacks at three in the morning. You cheat on your spouse. You snap at your kids. You quit listening to advice. You make bad decisions. You lose your happiness or your hope or your health.

I'm not being a doomsayer here—I'm just saying that I don't know what would have become of me if I had continued down a path of anger, loneliness, frustration, and emptiness. I don't think I would have liked the end of that path.

The key to change wasn't outside of me. It was within me.

It *was* me.

And it is you.

Sometimes when I talk to clients about recognizing and pursuing their wants, they tell me that it all sounds too good to be true. I get that. I remember feeling that way when people would encourage me to become an executive coach. It sounded like so much fun that I automatically assumed it was selfish. It was too good to be true, so I needed to set that idea aside, put my nose back to the grindstone, and be responsible.

I recall a client who was COO of a software company. He wanted to transition to being more involved in strategy, leadership development, and culture. Then he said, "That's not a real job description." He was discounting his want without even giving himself a chance to pursue it.

This is a common pattern I see with clients. Right after they finally express a bold new want, fear sneaks in to snuff it out. Be on the lookout if this happens after one of your new wants.

What's your dream? What seems too good to be true for you? Think about that for a minute. Imagine a lifestyle, a schedule, a job description, or an emotional state that you really would love to have, but it seems "too good to be true." This is intensely personal. What seems too good to be true to you might sound boring or terrifying to someone else, and that's okay. Remember, you don't have to justify your wants. But you do have to acknowledge them. Would you be willing to say your dream aloud now and let the want breathe? Would you be willing to ask for what you want and risk being disappointed?

Go ahead and speak it out loud: "A dream or want that I am aware of is _____."

Next, ask yourself: Why does it seem so good? What is so attractive to you? Why do you resonate with it? Why is it exciting and appealing? I want you to consider that maybe it feels so good to you because *it is so good* for you. Maybe "too good to be true" is telling you exactly where you're supposed to be.

Dig a little deeper. Why have you written that thing off? Why is it too good, too extravagant, too easy, too hard, too wonderful, too selfish, too much? What is the "too" that makes you turn away from the dream and settle for something mundane, constrictive, limiting?

An authenticity mindset means you pay attention to the stories you tell yourself and the excuses you make to give up too soon. What belief or story are you using to convince yourself that the things you want the most can't happen?

I can tell you why I wrote off my "too good to be true" for so long—a combination of fear and lack of self-worth. I didn't think I was worthy enough, and I didn't think I was good enough. I couldn't put words to it at first, so I settled for making excuses. But as I dug deeper into my mindsets and began to understand aliveness, the excuses were revealed for what they were.

If you want to understand yourself better, pay attention to what excites *and* what frustrates you. Your emotions are meant to work together, and they are meant to motivate you toward positive change. Too often we gaslight ourselves into doing what we don't want to do and not doing what we do want to do, then we wonder why we don't feel alive.

Aliveness is about reconnecting with your experience of life, and that begins with honesty. It's ok to admit that you are frustrated, bored, angry, hurt, lost, lonely, or scared. Those are normal human emotions, and they are helpful because they alert you to things that could be hurting you long-term. It is to be commended for wanting to feel happy, fulfilled, excited, motivated, whole, loved, and brave. These feelings are meant to encourage you to pursue the things that lead to long-term health.

I'm not saying to let your emotions control your decisions. Just because something feels uncomfortable doesn't make it wrong, and just because something is pleasurable in the moment doesn't make it right. We all understand that. I'm saying don't *live* by your feelings, but do *listen* to them.

Becoming a more authentic person is about more than just listening to your feelings. That's part of it, but authenticity is really about aligning all the parts of your life. That means learning to listen to yourself, being honest with yourself, and then taking actions that create inner alignment.

Guy and Katie Hendricks refer to this process of acting from a place of complete inner alignment as a "whole body yes." A whole body yes means your mind, emotions, will, and body are in complete alignment to a particular choice or action. It goes beyond duty and is characterized by genuine excitement and determination. This approach inspires individuals to honor their true selves by making choices that align with their innermost desires and values, thus fostering authenticity in their actions and decisions.

One way of viewing how we process information is to visualize three *centers of intelligence*: our head, our heart, and our gut. This concept was developed in part by Oscar Ichazo and Claudio Naranjo in their work on the Enneagram model, and it has been expanded and popularized by other writers and thinkers since then. These centers offer different perspectives and can tell us when we are in or out of alignment with who we really are.

Our *head* is best for processing data and information. We rely on our head when we want to include information as part of our decision or when we engage reasoning and logic. This center of intelligence gets a lot of attention and applause in modern society, but it's only part of how we perceive and evaluate information.

Our *heart* is best for processing relationships and emotions. When a decision has an emotional or relational component, we should consider what our heart wants. This center gets criticized sometimes because it's not "logical" or "data-driven." I'm all for logic and data, but I'm also convinced that our emotions and our interpersonal connections are invaluable, even if they can't be charted on a spreadsheet or flow chart.

Finally, our *gut* is best for processing sensations in our bodies. This is our intuition or our instincts. When we access our gut, we feel more grounded, connected, trusting, and confident. Again, this is less objective than data; and again, it often gets overlooked. And yet when you read the stories of great leaders or listen to them explain their process, they often come back to this point: you have to trust yourself. Often that means trusting your gut.

A fundamental aspect of aliveness is alignment in all three centers. The goal is to have your head, heart, and gut all aligned. On a practical level, I'm talking about alignment in your overall career and calendar. There might be moments where you have to do something you don't want to do or don't feel passionate about— that's a normal part of life. But the majority of your day should not be a constant tension or dissonance between these three centers. Rather, you should have alignment, and that alignment should spark greater aliveness.

I remember working with a business owner who was focused on opening multiple locations as quickly as possible to expand his reach. He had found what he thought to be the perfect location for one store. Rather than being excited, though, he noticed he felt some unease because the landlord was being difficult in their negotiations.

I asked him to recall what his Optimal State was, which we had discussed in a previous session. He said, "Freedom." As soon as he said it, he realized that if the landlord was difficult now, there would likely be more conflicts ahead during the course of the lease. He wanted a landlord who felt like a partner, not an adversary.

This landlord was not someone he wanted to enter a long-term relationship with.

Immediately he felt relieved. He passed on the location, and he soon found another location that was even better. In this situation, his authenticity helped him honor his internal resistance and become aligned. Instead of convincing himself to jump at the opportunity, he listened to his whole body and said no.

Helping people achieve alignment might be the single most important thing I do during coaching sessions. I don't tell them what to do. I give them feedback indicating whether I observe alignment or a lack of alignment. I hold up a mirror and let them define what they want and what they need to do to obtain that. I invite them to leave behind old ways of thinking that were short-circuiting their aliveness and to adopt new mindsets that empower and expand their aliveness.

When we do things out of obligation or because of old patterns, we easily lose alignment, which drains our energy and reduces our aliveness. On the other hand, when we are doing things that we truly love doing, things that are aligned with all three centers, we sense aliveness springing up within us. That's the sensation I want to experience every day.

We often say yes to requests from others because we want to be accepted, which is a core human need. Yet we rarely think of the cost, which includes not having time for the things that are a higher priority and/or things that help us feel alive. I love this sage advice often attributed to Warren Buffet: "The difference between successful people and really successful people is that really successful people say no to almost everything."

How about you? How aligned is your lifestyle with your head, heart, and gut? If you were to evaluate your calendar based on the energy you get from your various activities, are your choices coming from authenticity or from obligation?

Pay attention to your wants and your needs. Honor and respect your unhappiness. Be willing to question all your assumptions and make changes in any area. This is your life. You get only one! And nobody else can tell you how to live it.

As you wrestle with where you are and who you are today, and as you evaluate how to move forward into a more alive state, make sure to engage the tenacious side of you. I believe you have one, deep inside you. It's what has helped you overcome obstacle after obstacle and get to where you are now. Tap into that tenacity again. Whether it takes weeks, months, or years to discover the aliveness you dream of, it's worth it.

You are worth fighting for. So fight for true aliveness.

You are worth caring about. So care about what really matters.

You are worth listening to. So listen to your heart.

1. Write down five things you want (and haven't asked for yet). Don't censor yourself or judge yourself. Just write down what you want, big or small.

2. Do you notice any resistance or self-judgment surrounding the idea of asking for these things? List those thoughts and feelings. What do you think your judgments are based on?

3. Looking at that list, can you learn anything about yourself? What do you value? What are you missing? What would make you feel more alive?

4. What is one action you could take today to be more
   authentic, more aligned with who you are and what you
   want? In other words, if you were fully committed to
   feeling more alive, what would be the one action you
   would be doing?

5. What would your epitaph be if someone described your
   current approach to life? What do you want it to be?

10

OVERCOMING FEAR ALIVENESS MINDSET 5: COURAGE

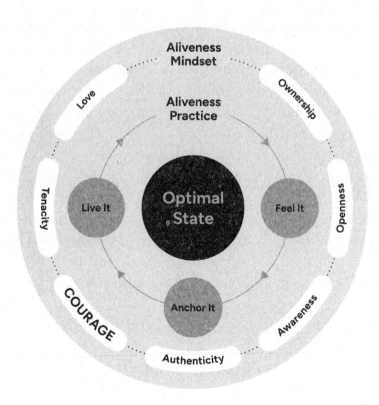

CHARLIE WAS A SERIAL HEALTH-CARE ENTREPRENEUR WHO HAD EXPE-rienced significant transformational success in his business endeavors. In a coaching session, he told me he was contemplating what to do next. He expressed to me that he wanted to do something bigger, something that would make a difference. But he didn't know what that would look like.

So I asked him a simple question: "What are your goals?"

Charlie froze. He didn't even know where to begin. As we talked further, it became clear that the reason he had locked up was fear and anxiety. Despite his past success, he was afraid of the future. Afraid of failure. Afraid of dreaming about what he most wanted and not being successful.

It didn't surprise me. I've experienced that exact feeling, and you probably have too. What if your success was luck? What if it was a one-hit wonder? What if it was due to the economy, your team, good fortune, competitor's mistakes, or some other factor? When I contemplated leaving my company and launching a coaching business, I remember thinking, *What if I fail and I have to go back to my old life, working for someone else in the industry I wanted to leave?* It was an intimidating thought, and it kept me from moving forward for quite some time.

For Charlie, the fear had arisen during the liminal space before his next goal. It was during the transition after one victory had been won but the next was far from certain. Navigating this in-between place can prove challenging. Author and speaker Victoria Labalme refers to life transitions as the "Fog of Not Knowing." Insightfully, Labalme writes, "At the edge of not knowing is the beginning of the extraordinary."[25]

This required Charlie to have courage to forge ahead without a clear path or a definitive plan. Not courage in the sense of charging headfirst into battle like some Roman gladiator, but courage in being okay with the unknown. Courage to move forward even without knowing when or if the next big idea would come. Courage to acknowledge his fallibility and uncertainty of life without being paralyzed by it.

In our coaching session, instead of trying to create goals, I asked him, "What lights you up? What gets you excited?"

He said, "Helping people feel healthier and live longer." We talked about what that might look like. He began to dream about perfecting his health-care model in his city and then scaling it across the country. Within thirty minutes, he was calculating how many patients each doctor could serve and how many would need to work at each site.

We didn't frame all of this as his goals. We framed it as his *mission*. He was simply aligning his actions with who he truly was and where he felt most alive.

By the time we ended our session, he had a clearer vision of what was ahead. More importantly, he had tamed his fears enough to see past them. Notice that the change in Charlie's attitude didn't start by listing goals and brainstorming strategies. It started with his mindset. It started with ownership, openness, awareness, authenticity, and *courage* to move forward. He acknowledged his fears, but then he tapped into the courage that comes from alignment.

Remember, you can't eradicate fear and anxiety, so don't make that your focus. Instead, listen to them long enough to learn from them, to hear what they are trying to tell you—then choose courage.

The ambiguity of life means that in order to achieve and remain in a state of aliveness, you will always need courage. That's why I've included it as one of the individual mindsets that make up the Aliveness Mindset. You'll grow in it, but you'll never outgrow it, because life is always bigger than our capacity to control or understand it. Making peace with that reality, and moving forward in light of it, is courage.

I love this statement that is often attributed to Victor Frankl: "Between stimulus and response lies a space. In that space lie our freedom and power to choose a response. In our response lies our growth and our happiness."[26]

Charlie was in that space. I've been in that space. I'm sure you have too. You might even be there now. It's the "space between." It's the space where you have freedom and power to decide whether you are going to fall back in fear or move forward in faith.

Faith in what?

Mostly, faith in yourself.

What else do you have? You might believe in a higher power, or in karma, or in fate, and that's fine. I have deep respect for various belief systems, as long as they're not hurting people. But regardless of your spiritual or philosophical convictions, at the end of the day, all you can really *control* is yourself.

And that's a powerful force indeed.

Courage, for me, is the willingness to carry your full self into an uncertain future. As Brené Brown has written, "Courage is where vulnerability and fear meet."[27] You can't guarantee success, but what is success anyway? You can't guarantee you won't fail, but isn't failure an inescapable part of being human? You can't predict the outcome, but isn't that the essence of adventure?

Of course, I didn't always think this way. I remember being in San Diego at another CLG retreat, in January 2013. This was months into my aliveness journey, but I was dragging my feet when it came to making tough decisions relating to my CEO role. In a room full of participants, Diana called me out. By this time we were all very close, and she knew exactly what I was facing—and what I was avoiding.

"Jack," she said, "honestly, I hope your company goes out of business. That would be the best thing that could happen to you. You are only running it out of obligation. It's blocking your aliveness."

The whole room looked at me to see my response. My initial reaction was rage. My inner dialogue went something like this: *Who the hell are you to wish that the second-generation family business that my father started, my livelihood, and the livelihood of all our employees would go away?*

Underneath my anger, though, was crippling fear and anxiety. My stomach felt like a seized engine. I walked down to the beach and sat there for an hour, staring at the ocean. I was fucking terrified. I was afraid that if I gave up on myself now, I would never become fully alive. I had glimpsed enough to know I wanted it, but fear and anxiety were holding me back, and I was the only one who could do anything about that.

I knew that there was truth in what was said. I was scared of what I needed to face to experience more aliveness. There were conversations I still had been avoiding—with my siblings, our employees, and my wife. My mind raced. What would I do next? How would I make money to support my family? Good fathers are providers, right? And what would happen to all of the employees?

A mix of courage and resolve rose up inside me. I realized something: *courage in the face of difficulty was part of my aliveness.*

· · · · · · · · · · ·

Courage in the face of difficulty

was part of my aliveness.

· · · · · · · · · · ·

I had been waiting for fear to be gone before I would let myself feel alive, but aliveness transcends fear. If anything, aliveness is energized by fear because you can be courageous only in the face of risk, and those moments of boldness are often when you live most freely and authentically. I chose courage that day. And I've chosen it a thousand times since, because courage is a mindset and a lifestyle, not a momentary flash of adrenaline.

I wish I could say that I instantly knew what to do, that I went home and did it, and that everything was resolved in a month. But that's not how it worked for me, and it's not how it works for most people. Your aliveness journey is probably going to be messier than that. There is a lot of self-reflection, a lot of trial and error, a lot of learning and unlearning.

All I knew was that my current way of living was not what I needed or wanted to carry forward. But the future was uncertain, and uncertainty can be terrifying. And that's exactly where courage is needed the most. Finding aliveness is a lifelong pursuit, and you have to be willing to stay the course.

What does courage look like for you, and where do you need to engage it? That's the real question here. I share my journey only to help you reflect on yours. If you are serious about experiencing aliveness, you'll need to choose courage time and time again. That will look different for you than for me, or for Charlie, or for others whose stories I've shared. It will even look different depending on the time of your life or the situation you're facing.

Don't confuse courage with adrenaline. Some people live on adrenaline, and they think the rush they feel when they make a bold move is aliveness. Adrenaline provides a short-term energy that is meant for survival, and the driving force behind it is often fear. As a long-term strategy, adrenaline will usually leave you feeling spent and burnt out.

In contrast, aliveness feels more like effortless play. We have infinite energy when we are alive, and courage is a natural result. That's what Charlie experienced. When he aligned his head, heart, and gut, courage began to flow freely. He still faced risk, but he felt excited and drawn to the challenge.

That's the kind of courage you should strive for: one that flows easily and naturally from within you. I'm not saying it will be easy to make the right choice every time, but courage is within you, just as aliveness is, because courage is part of your aliveness.

Reactivity, on the other hand, will stop the flow of courage. If you find yourself responding in a toxic way to a situation at work, evaluate your reactivity level. Do you feel threatened by something? Are you afraid of losing something or failing someone?

A client named Cheryl said that she would find herself in a reactive state every time John, the COO, informed her there were issues in shipping out products. She had recently snapped at him and told him to just handle any issues and not get her involved. When she did, John fell quiet. He was clearly surprised by Cheryl's intense reaction because he was just doing his job by looping her in on issues.

Cheryl admitted to me that she'd overreacted. I asked her to take a breath and think of her Optimal State, which was "Confidence." She took a moment to reduce her reactivity and focus on that word. Then I asked, "What emotion might be underneath your anger?"

It took only a couple of seconds for Cheryl to realize that her anger and judgment of John were disguising her underlying emotion of fear. Her company had missed Q1 sales numbers, and she feared not hitting Q2 sales numbers. His comments triggered fear associated with her need for security. The problem wasn't John: it was her reactive response to a normal fear and a real human need.

As I've mentioned, reactivity is often tied to the core human needs of approval, control, and security. Crystalizing the true source of reactivity in a nonjudgmental way is an important step to returning to aliveness.

The issue in Cheryl's mind shifted from "John's behavior triggered my anger" to "I'm scared we are going to miss our sales numbers." This realization helped Cheryl regain her confidence. She felt calmer and was able to see the issues more clearly. She met with John and apologized for getting reactive. They worked together to resolve the shipping problems and create a strategy to increase shipments and sales.

Notice that once her reactivity was lowered, fear was no longer an obstacle. It was there, but it was just a reality, not a controlling factor. Courage naturally rose to the surface, communication improved, and creativity returned.

Let me say one last thing about fear and courage: fear is sneaky. It can masquerade as an obstacle or excuse. "I'm not going to have that tough conversation because that leader would get demotivated." You think, *It's no use.* You decide, "I don't have..." or "I can't..." and your brain fills in the blanks without conscious effort.

When I was wrestling with my decision to step down and shutter the company, I struggled for a long time because I thought it was safer to be miserable in the known than to risk stepping into the unknown. That's the paralyzing power of fear and anxiety. Plus, it was easier to blame others for getting in the way of my happiness rather than to take action on what I wanted and risk not succeeding.

That's the paradox of becoming alive. You have to shed a few things along the way: things like security, certainty, and comfort. Not that I was secure, certain, or comfortable before. I wasn't. But at least it was a familiar misery.

In my case, the breaking point came when things at work were becoming increasingly untenable and the company's performance was suffering. I realized that my retirement and the investment I was making in the company were at risk. I was willing to be unhappy at work, but I was not willing to pay for any future losses or compromise my family's future. I was done. I was finally able to give myself permission to make the changes I knew I needed to make.

In retrospect, I wish I would have realized I didn't need "permission." I didn't need to wait until financial threats forced me to make a change I knew I needed to make anyway if I was going to be truly alive. But I had allowed fear and anxiety to convince me that I couldn't leave without a clear, compelling reason.

I don't blame myself for taking that long. I had a lot of issues to deal with inside me. I had to figure out what I wanted, what I was good at, and what a truly alive Jack might look like. I had to overcome fear, anxiety, insecurity, a savior complex, and a too-high reliance on what other people thought. I didn't want to hurt anyone in the pursuit of my own dream, including my family and employees, and I didn't want to risk my family's financial stability.

At the same time, why did I feel like I needed "permission" to quit? It's my life. And I'm a grown-ass adult. Shouldn't I be the one who gives myself permission to do what I know I need to do?

And shouldn't *you*?

Of course you should. But it takes a mindset of courage. And sometimes you have to change a few other wrong mindsets before courage is even an option.

I don't judge myself, and I don't judge anyone I coach. We're all on our own journey. I tell clients, and I'm going to tell you as well: *You don't need anyone's permission to take charge of your own aliveness.* You don't need an excuse to quit things that are harmful. You don't need twenty-seven bulletproof reasons to make changes that you already know will be healthy and helpful. It's your life, and you don't have to justify everything you do to anyone else. You don't have to take care of yourself only as a last resort.

Of course you should be careful and wise with any changes you make. Take your time. Consider the implications. Think of all the people who might be affected. I support getting out of your comfort zone, but do it in a way that feels friendly to you. It should be a healthy stretch. I don't recommend doing anything that feels terrifying.

My guess is that you already consider the implications of change. Maybe too much. There's a difference between considering real implications and being overly attached to a story you're telling yourself about what others will think or how they'll react.

Maybe you need to give yourself permission to quit some things, start some things, and tweak some things. To explore. To admit your desires. To redefine your role. To adjust the expectations others have of you and expectations you have of yourself.

No one else can give you permission to be yourself. You have to do that.

But it takes courage.

1. How would you define courage? Can you think of a time you demonstrated a courageous mindset? Did you feel alive? How would you describe the feeling? What helped you take action in that moment?

2. Why do you think courage is important to aliveness?

3. Where are you procrastinating, feeling stuck, or avoiding taking action? What is one courageous thing you could do today to take a step toward aliveness? It can be a small, "hop over the fence" (easily attainable) goal.

PLAY THE LONG GAME
ALIVENESS MINDSET 6:
TENACITY

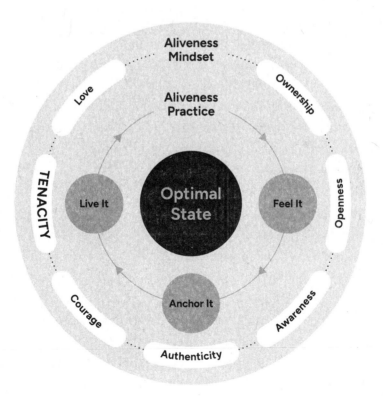

PAUL, ONE OF MY CLIENTS WHO HAS BEEN WITH ME THE LONGEST, runs a successful advertising company. In the beginning, his focus in our sessions was on gaining confidence and clarity to grow his company and lead his team. His company's revenues grew every year for five consecutive years. In year six, his business exploded, and revenue tripled from the previous record year. The business had grown to a size he couldn't have imagined when he started.

He began working even harder to keep up with the demand. He loved what he and his team had created. They efficiently planned every day to the fullest. Increased work hours became the new norm. Paul didn't mind it, though, because his work had value. He was thinking how much bigger he could grow his company.

Then disaster struck.

A large client decided not to renew an agreement with Paul's company. This was common in his industry, but it hit Paul hard. Suddenly, his full calendar was 30 percent less full. He had lots of free time. Rather than embrace the freedom and extra time in his calendar, Paul spiraled into a dark place. He began to question his self-worth. He had a harder time trusting himself. He lost his confidence. He blamed himself and others.

Before I tell you the rest of the story, let me emphasize that Paul was committed to his aliveness. He had been practicing tools for years, and he was good at it. That's important, because aliveness is not a quick fix for a bad day. Aliveness is a way of life. And sometimes, you have to really fight for it.

You have to be *tenacious*.

Tenacity is the quality of being persistent, determined, and unwilling to give up or be discouraged in the face of challenges or obstacles. When it comes to aliveness, a tenacious mindset is one that has a strong and unwavering commitment to remaining in aliveness—or to recovering it if it's been lost.

Paul was trying to get his aliveness back.

Over the years we had worked together, Paul had become familiar with a number of tools that helped him remain in his Optimal State. I call these Living All In (LAI) tools. I didn't invent these tools any more than a carpenter invents the tools he or she uses; but they are part of my tool kit, and they are part of Paul's, and they can be part of yours. I'll explain many of them in greater detail in chapter 18.

Paul had become very efficient at accessing his OS whenever he had an issue by using two or three LAI tools. This time, none of the tools were working for him. His dark state lasted for days, then weeks, then months, which had never happened before.

Paul reached out to me and asked for an extended coaching session. When he arrived, he looked stressed and gaunt. He was locked in fear, and he was fixated on regaining the "lost" revenue from his company's peak as quickly as possible.

I asked Paul when he'd last felt this anxious. He said it was about a decade ago, when his last business was floundering. Paul knew that on a rational level, he shouldn't be this worried just because one client didn't renew. However, his body was reacting as if he were reliving the traumatic experience years ago when his prior company was losing money.

I suggested that he could narrow his focus and bring the goalposts closer. Instead of seeking to return to his OS, his goal should be to get unstuck, even just a little.

We did some breathing and meditation to calm his nervous system. I reminded Paul we were looking for small wins. Using questions, I walked him through steps to increase his openness and awareness and feel all of his emotions. "Are you resisting? Where in your body do you feel this resistance? Could you be okay with allowing these sensations to simply exist? Could you acknowledge and accept the fear-based thoughts and the feeling of being stuck? Could you show yourself self-compassion rather than judgment?" After a few minutes, he was visibly calmer. I could see in his face and tone that his inner dialogue was beginning to shift away from reactivity.

I thought the best approach for someone with Paul's mastery of tools would be for him to coach himself. I had him practice self-distancing, which is a great tool to assess a situation with less emotion.

Author and psychologist Ethan Kross refers to this psychological distancing as the brain's ability to "zoom out." Often, when faced with a problem, we tend to lose sight of the bigger picture. Being too close to the situation narrows our perspective, leading to feeling overwhelmed and triggering stress responses that flood our bodies with adrenaline, cortisol, and negativity. This is where the practice of zooming out becomes valuable. While it doesn't magically solve our problems, it effectively calms the mental chatter, enabling us to think more clearly and authentically.[28]

To help Paul zoom out, I asked him how he would coach a best friend going through the same experience. He suggested a variety of LAI tools to be used throughout the day. I took notes, then I gave him the list. That became his aliveness plan.

- He would begin each day with gratitude for feeling alive.
- He would look at the pictures on his Wall of Gratitude, which was a collection of curated pictures that best reflected his feeling of aliveness.
- He would meditate regularly to calm his nervous system and ground himself.
- He would focus on deep belly breathing throughout the day since he noticed that his breathing was shortened when he was stressed.
- He would schedule calendar reminders to repeat his Optimal State and his Anchoring Mindsets aloud four

to six times per day. (We'll talk more about Anchoring Mindsets in chapter 14.)
- He committed to taking his kids to school to connect with them before he began his day.
- When he noticed fear-based thoughts, he would reframe his thinking and practice self-compassion.

It was a great plan. I was impressed. He committed to the plan he suggested, and I offered support. Our goal was to chip away at his feeling stuck and to achieve a more positive mood and mindset. I wanted him to access the aliveness and creativity that were always within him, but it wouldn't happen overnight.

Over the next few days, he added more tools to his plan.
- He set aside time to be creative. He sat in a comfortable room, put on his favorite songs, and focused on reflection and creativity.
- He journaled about what he was thinking and feeling to provide greater self-distancing and metacognition.
- He used reframing to minimize his negative thoughts, and he repeated key words, or "magic words," to loosen the grip of fear and anxiety (see chapter 18 for an explanation of this tool).
- He used positive affirmations: "I always figure it out. I love what I do. My work is impactful. I am resilient."

In one week, he made a great deal of progress. He realized that underneath his fear of lost business was unprocessed sadness about not working with the dynamic leaders in the company that did not renew. He would really miss them. He allowed himself to grieve. By fully feeling his emotions, he opened up more space inside himself. He felt lighter.

He also realized he was unconsciously blocking his own aliveness. He was resisting everything that had happened: the client that didn't renew; his reaction; his emotions of fear, anger, and sadness; and his inability to get unstuck.

The following week we added more practices. We did what I call a Look Back exercise. If he were to look back at himself ten years ago and ask that person what he thought about the accomplishments of the Paul of today, what would he say? He answered, "Exceeded expectations! I would be proud of how I created the new company." We let those thoughts and feelings sink in for a few moments.

He also spent time reviewing a note on his phone where he had kept a record of texts and emails from clients praising his work. This was something he had started collecting long before this moment, and reviewing the positive feedback was effective in helping him get his self-confidence back in a healthy place.

All of these tools were intended to empower Paul to believe that he could get *himself* unstuck. Aliveness was inside him. He didn't need to land the next client before he could change how he felt. Our goal was to continue to chip away at his fear and find more space to feel confident and calm.

Each week Paul felt more relaxed and had greater energy. He went from brief moments of being back in his OS to extended periods of time. Then, he felt a huge wave of creativity and flow begin. He met with his team and shared his new ideas. Together, they developed several strategies to grow their business. Paul and his team were re-energized, and he was back to his old self.

I shared so much of Paul's story here because I find it both inspiring and informative. He refused to stay stuck not only in his business but in his mind too. He recognized that the real battle was within him and that the solution was there as well. And he was willing to do whatever it took to get his aliveness back.

In the pursuit of aliveness, you have to play the long game. You can't expect quick fixes or easy answers because usually the things that need to change are within you, and that kind of soul-searching and honesty doesn't happen without some resistance. However, when you keep going, when you persevere through the low moments, the transformation you experience is real. That is what is so powerful about aliveness. The very pursuit of it changes you from the inside out.

· · · · · · · · · · ·

In the pursuit of aliveness, you have to play the long game.

· · · · · · · · · · ·

Aliveness is more of a marathon than a sprint, and that's why tenacity is required. In a marathon or triathlon, there are usually multiple moments when you want to quit, when you think your body can't take any more. Good athletes know that, and they go into the race mentally prepared for it. In those moments of self-doubt, your mind can be your worst enemy or your best friend. It can work against you or work for you. It all depends on your mindset.

The same goes for learning to live in aliveness. There will be moments when you think, *This isn't possible. This isn't worth it. This is too hard. Maybe I should settle for "good enough" or "it isn't that bad." Maybe I should quit dreaming about something greater and just resign myself to the rat race.*

In those moments, you have to engage tenacity. Hold on to your strong, unwavering commitment to yourself: to the life you want, the life you need, the life you deserve, and the life you were built for. You might feel stuck now, but you can find your way back to freedom.

By the way, the wave of creativity Paul experienced after being stuck is common. It is similar to the phenomenon of a second wind when you are running or biking. Just when you feel like you can't continue, there is often a breakthrough, a new burst of energy, and you hit your stride like never before. When you feel stuck, it can be encouraging to remind yourself that a breakthrough of creativity could be just ahead.

I like to think of tenacity as being similar to having grit. Angela Duckworth, a psychologist and researcher, has extensively studied the concept of grit. She describes it as the passion and persever-ance someone has for long-term goals. Grit means staying consis-tent and not giving up, even when facing challenges.[29] Sometimes, being tenacious just means showing up again and again.

When researchers studied a group of surgical residents, they found that those with more grit from the start had much better mental well-being after six months compared to those with less grit. The study showed that having grit not only predicts posi-tive mental health but also helps improve well-being over time, reducing the risk of burnout.[30]

The key is to not give up. Keep moving. Keep trying. You don't have to experience total aliveness overnight, but you can take a tiny step in the right direction. That starts within you, though: it's a mindset you choose to adopt.

Sometimes I use the word *devotion* to communicate this unwavering commitment to aliveness. The term *devotion* may feel more at home in romantic or religious settings than in a book on leadership development. Maybe that's why I like it—because it goes beneath the surface and speaks about *heart*. It implies emotion, passion, loyalty, and dogged commitment to the goal of being fully alive. Devotion to myself. Devotion to my potential and my capacity. Devotion to what I can accomplish and to the impact I can have on those around me. Devotion to being really, truly, fully alive.

It's right to feel passionate about personal growth. This is your life. If you're going to be passionate, loyal, emotional, and committed to something, shouldn't it be to *you*?

We've been conditioned to think it's normal to be driven by the bottom line and that self-care and personal growth are unnecessary luxuries. We've learned to be passionate about profits but passive about our personal goals. We're faithful to our job descriptions but often unfaithful to our mental health and work-life balance.

I'm not saying to stop being committed to your work, but I am saying it's okay to get a little intense, a little aggressive, even ruthless about what you need and want. You know that nagging feeling inside that something is missing? That frustration with the status quo? That sense of feeling stuck? Those feelings are trying to tell you something about you. They're telling you that you'd better take a look at the balance sheet of your soul, the profit and loss report of your mind, with the same urgency that you do your business.

That's why you have to go all in to make this work. Not all in on a method, but all in on *yourself*.

Back when I was taking tentative steps toward coaching, a friend and YPO forum member at the time, Andrew Swinand, said that All In is my mentality. My body lit up. All In describes my approach to everything I do in life. It's what I expect from my clients too: that they be all in on their commitment to themselves.

That is devotion. That is tenacity.

See the parallel between tenacity in *aliveness* and tenacity in your *career*. Too often we are willing to go all in for our career, for profits, or for growth, but we don't give ourselves permission to apply that same tenacity to our aliveness.

Leaders I work with are very strong, effective, committed people. But often, they don't put in the work on themselves. They don't include their aliveness within their definition of success.

That's the first work you need to do.

How about you? Are you committed to being more alive? Are you determined to bring the best version of yourself into your day-to-day experience?

Are you *all in*?

---

1. Would you consider yourself a tenacious person? Can you think of a time you demonstrated tenacity toward creating greater aliveness for yourself?

2. On a scale of 1–10, what is your level of tenacity toward your own aliveness? What would help you get to a 10?

3. Can you think of a time when you struggled to believe in yourself or when you felt stuck? Where you were watching from the stands rather than "in the arena" striving valiantly?[31] How did you get out of that funk?

4. What would it mean to be devoted to yourself?

5. What areas of your life require you to have a tenacious mindset today?

12

CONNECTION IS EVERYTHING ALIVENESS MINDSET 7: LOVE

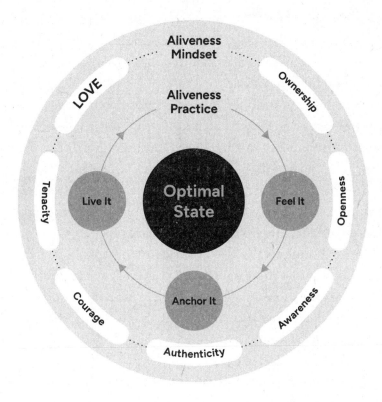

EARLIER I MENTIONED CHARLIE, A DOCTOR WHO RAN A SUCCESSFUL medical practice during the pandemic and was trying to decide how to next grow his business. Eventually he settled on creating a vitality and longevity clinic, with the goal of branching out to other cities as well.

For Charlie, one of the most impactful aspects of his original health-care business was how he was able to serve and support his community. So when he began contemplating what to do next, "giving back" was high on his priority list. He told me that in the past, his focus had been on making money. Now, he wanted to have an impact. He was on a mission to improve health care and make it more accessible and effective while helping his patients enjoy healthier lives. He wanted to create a more caring, loving environment for his team by empowering them to realize their dreams for themselves and their families. And he wanted to be present for his wife and kids.

He would make money, but money was not his driver. Sharing love was his driver. He was catching a vision not just for economic opportunity but for sharing, giving, and serving. Today, he has one clinic up and running, and he's envisioning more. He's also continuing to evaluate how he can share more of himself and what matters to him with others. He's actively exploring ways to incorporate that into his business endeavors.

When I think back to what struck him most about our conversation, it was that these are all opportunities for him to share his love. That's the motivating force. When he was evaluating his next steps, he knew that if it wasn't about helping, giving, sharing, and empowering, he didn't want to do it.

He had a mindset of *love*.

Love is not a word you hear very often in the business world. We talk about loving products or loving ideas, maybe, but loving *people* is not often discussed. I think that needs to change. We all need love, and we all know when we're loved. It's unspoken, but it's not unfelt, and it can make all the difference in any work relationship.

A mindset of love is about more than having warm, fuzzy feelings toward people. Author Bell Hooks wrote, "Affection is only one ingredient of love. To truly love we must learn to mix various ingredients—care, affection, recognition, respect, commitment, and trust, as well as honest and open communication."[32] All of those things are invaluable in the workplace, and all of them are perceived by the people we show them to, whether they are called "love" or not.

When it comes to aliveness, the concept of a love mindset is one I've been exploring a lot. Can you be truly alive if you don't love? Can you bring the best version of yourself into your day-to-day experience if you don't give or receive love?

I don't think you can.

Humans are social creatures. We don't do well on our own. I know some people are more introverted than others, and some people have a smaller social battery that needs to be recharged more often. But we all need to be connected, and love is first and foremost about connection and relationships.

Earlier I referenced the famous Harvard study on human satisfaction, happiness, and flourishing that Robert Waldinger and Marc Schulz evaluate in their book *The Good Life*. Waldinger and Schulz state, "When we really think about the consistent signal that comes through after eighty-four years of study and hundreds of research papers, it is that one simple message: Positive relationships are essential to human well-being."[33]

Complexity experts Jennifer Garvey Berger and Carolyn Coughlin describe love as a "genius" leadership skill. They argue that in modern organizations, *connections* hold greater significance than the *competence* of any one person. Therefore, building

thriving systems is possible only through high-quality connections. That's where love comes in. Loving relationships help reduce
loneliness and isolation and meet the innate human longing to be
deeply connected with those around us.[34]

When I consider my own experience, one of the things that
most affected my aliveness as a leader was the transactional nature
of the industry I was in. I experienced many times that no matter
your relationship to the customer, price was the ultimate factor.
Even a penny difference could lose a sale.

As I was discovering aliveness for myself, I frequently shared
stories with my customers about what I was learning and incorpo-
rating into my life. They would often call or text me later to say I
had helped them with their own issues. I started to notice that these
conversations were far more interesting to me than typical conversations related to products for their stores. We talked about our fears,
what we most wanted in life, and what was getting in the way. During
our conversations we would all be more vulnerable and authentic. I
felt more connected to people I had known for two decades. Our relationship no longer felt transactional. It felt meaningful.

Maybe you wouldn't call that love, but it is connection. It's
care and concern that is shared, felt, and valued.

I didn't realize it at the time, but one of the things that was
missing in my work was love. I'm not blaming that on everyone
else, or even on me—I think that it would have been difficult for
me to create an atmosphere of love in a job that was not a good fit
for me on so many levels. But in my current role, as I consider my
clients, what I do is truly an act of love. It's relational. I care about
them and their success. My input into their lives is a way of saying,
"I care about you. I love you."

Of course they pay me, just like your clients and customers
pay you. But that doesn't mean there isn't love built into the

relationship. Care and concern for others are not at odds with business. Actually, I think they make great business sense.

Of course, you don't have to state your love to show it. I'm not on a campaign to get bosses to say "I love you" to their workers. But I do think your day-to-day experience, even at work, should include a heart component if you are going to bring the best version of yourself into every aspect of your life.

In your pursuit of aliveness, include your heart. Don't neglect this vital element of human connection and interdependency. Be intentional about leaning into love, into generosity, into sharing, into connection. I believe it will only contribute to your aliveness.

Why does love matter so much? We often think of it as a touchy-feely emotion, as something soft and almost weak. In reality, a mindset of love is actually a strong, effective protection against some of the pitfalls that could threaten your aliveness. Let's look at a few of the ways love can help protect you.

1. Love is a protection against ego.

Leading with your ego is generally a terrible idea. You might be able to get people to follow you for a while, but at what cost? Often, one of the costs is your aliveness. It's impossible to achieve true aliveness if you're always propping up a flimsy ego. On the other hand, if you embrace true humility, you will be able to practice the ownership, openness, awareness, and authenticity necessary to walk in who you are truly meant to be.

Love counteracts ego by reminding you that everyone matters. That includes you. When you love and accept others, you more easily love and accept yourself. And when you care for yourself, you have a greater capacity to care for others. It's always both/and rather than either/or.

2. Love is a protection against isolation.

Leading can be a lonely place at times, but it doesn't have to be as lonely as we sometimes make it. Often some of the isolation leaders experience is self-imposed. It stems, at least in part, from a self-protective tendency.

I get that. You have too many demands and too little time. You are always letting someone down, no matter how hard you try. You might even be afraid of getting too close to someone because you have to fire them. With all this pressure, it can seem easier to shut yourself off from the world. I call this a bunker mentality. In my case, the more stress and pressure I felt, the more I isolated myself and the longer the hours I worked. The same is true for many of my clients.

Don't let pressure push you away from people. You need relationships. You need support. You need a team. You need to include people in your life, and love will help bring that about.

3. Love is a protection against fear and anxiety.

We've seen how dangerous and subversive reactivity can be. Living with untamed fear and anxiety makes entering into aliveness difficult, if not impossible.

Love has a way of disarming fear. Not all fears, of course, but many of them. How? For one thing, it helps you see what's truly important. Love provides perspective. It reminds you of what really matters in life, and often that comes down to people. It's so easy to get in your own head, caught up in anxiety about things that may or may not happen. Focusing on real people is a way to ground yourself in what matters most.

Love also overcomes fear by giving you something tangible to do that produces positive feelings. When you are generous, or when you are caring, or when you consider the needs of someone else, you get instant, positive, emotional feedback from your own brain. You remind yourself that you matter, that you are good, and that you are making a difference. When you find yourself in a state of reactivity triggered by fear or anxiety, take a moment to consider ways to help and serve others. This is a proactive way to defuse the fight-or-flight response, become conscious of your reactions, and take intentional steps in the right direction.

Again, you don't need to tell your team how much you love them every day or include heart emojis in all your DM messages. You can show love through actions and words that are natural and comfortable to you. You might use words like *friendship, caring, concern, commitment,* and *teamwork.* But more than words, culti-vate a *mindset* within yourself. Not a set of best practices or lead-ership strategies, but ways of thinking that are transformative and that will produce aliveness within you. The goal is to have genuine care and concern for other people and to let that mindset help shape your leadership.

I remember working with Bill, the CEO of a retail chain who often found himself getting distracted during his one-on-ones with his team. He usually started feeling antsy about forty-five minutes into his sixty-minute meetings, and he would keep checking his phone and losing interest.

This behavior is not what he wanted for himself or his employees. He wanted them to know that he was fully engaged and present. He wanted them to feel heard, valued, and cared for. Bill didn't just want to seem interested. He wanted to *be* interested. These were key team members who mattered to him.

We discussed an LAI tool I referenced earlier called the *magic word,* which refers to choosing a specific term that reminds you to change an attitude or behavior. The goal is to find a word or phrase that will help you show up the way you want in a partic-ular scenario. He picked the word *savor.* Whenever he felt the first pangs of distraction, he would silently say the word *savor* to himself. Savor didn't mean "fake it." It meant "enjoy it." It was a reminder to Bill that he wanted to connect with people because he cared about them and what they had to say.

Every time Bill said his magic word, he could feel himself relax both physically and mentally. He was able to remain present with his team members, which made them feel more cared for and made Bill feel like he was bringing the best version of himself to the situation. Bill was demonstrating a loving mindset. I don't think we used the term *love* even once in our conversations, but it was apparent in his approach to everything he did. He kept the human element at the forefront, and it contributed to his aliveness as well as to his effectiveness as a leader. Bill realized something significant when he was able to savor the time with members of his team: They noticed he was more present with them. They noticed that he was giving them his *full* attention.

Attention is love.

Some leaders resist showing or expressing love in ways that make them uncomfortable. That's okay. Most of those leaders resonate with the idea that they can show their love by giving their teams their full, undivided attention.

I can think of example after example of leaders who demonstrate a loving mindset. One leader who comes to mind knows so much about his team's personal lives that he encourages them to go home to attend to personal issues when they flare up—such as an aging parent, a sick child, or even a pet emergency—and makes sure that others on the team pick up the slack.

Another leader I work with realized during COVID-19 that her company no longer needed to rent office space. They went fully remote, saving the company over one hundred thousand dollars per year. To give back, every year she takes the entire company on vacation to relax, bond, and feel appreciated.

Love can be present even when a leader must be let go. Another client, Rhonda, along with her senior leadership team, had hired an executive team leader. After a year, it was clear the new hire was not the best fit. Rhonda's team had several conversations with the leader about where he was falling short, and they expressed their concern that the leader did not seem to be open to feedback and that his team had lost faith in him.

The senior team ultimately made the decision to let the leader go. This was the result of shared learning and alignment. They approached a hard thing—termination of an executive leader—with a wise, loving mindset. They treated it as an opportunity for everyone involved. They were transparent with the leader and the company about what happened. It was a graceful exit, and the leader was given a chance to say goodbye. His former team was actually energized by the experience.

Often when someone is let go, there is a lot of fear that "I could be next." In this instance, the executive team minimized that potential reaction by demonstrating compassionate leadership, which resulted in faith, not fear.

Not only is it important to have a mindset that gives love, you also need to be able to receive love. Sometimes high-functioning leaders struggle with this. You might be used to being the strong one, the wise voice, the protector, the provider. But you have needs too, like any human. You need acceptance, approval, companion-ship, support, grace, encouragement.

When you are committed to aliveness, it is more important than ever to be loved because the journey is not always easy. It is messy at times, and messiness equates to vulnerability. You need to see yourself not only as capable of loving but as worthy of love.

After I attended many leadership trainings, I became more aware of my reactivity and how closed I could be to feedback. That was incredibly painful at times. It wasn't easy to hear how my reactivity impacted Judy and the family. Yet I felt more connected to them when they were more candid with me about my negative behaviors. I knew I was loved even when I was being challenged. As a matter of fact, I knew I was loved *because* I was being challenged. They truly wanted to see the best version of me rise to the surface.

When I first began understanding aliveness, it caused some ripples in my marriage. Even though Judy and I were both exploring consciousness, I worried about whether we were growing together or apart. I found myself wondering, *Am I the same person that she married and raised our kids with? Will she want this new version of Jack?* I never stopped loving her, but the questions and fears were real.

To Judy, some of the changes were unsettling. I was meeting new people and sharing my deepest thoughts. I was more focused on myself than I had been before. All of this was challenging after twenty years of marriage. *She never stopped loving me.* While at times she wondered what our future together would look like, she also recognized that my journey was good not only for my growth but also for hers. We had many discussions about our different experiences and about affirming our intentions to be together. It was still a challenging time, but our relationship and marriage is stronger and more honest than ever. We have learned how to honor our own and each other's experiences and speak our truths.

The same is true with my relationship today with our three now adult daughters. They are all amazing women in their own ways, and I am incredibly proud of them. I am also grateful for the depth of our connection. I really enjoy our time together, whatever we are doing. I know that if I'm not present when I'm with them, they will feel comfortable to give me that feedback (and they have!). I encourage them to be fully candid and authentic with me, both in terms of love and appreciation as well as when they are disappointed or frustrated with me. It is because we are all authentic that I feel more love and appreciation. I know that each of them feels the same way.

I was fortunate to have had support from my family and close friends. I was supported, encouraged, accepted, and loved when I needed it most. I don't know if I could have done it otherwise. I needed people then, and I need people now, and I know they need me. I would not have been able to push myself the way I did without Judy's unwavering support and faith in me. During the transition, we had to drastically cut our budget. Judy was the first to volunteer to cut expenses while trying to minimize the impact it would have on our kids. I needed people I could rely on to encourage me or challenge me to move forward, and Judy was my number one cheerleader. She allowed me the time I needed to pursue my personal and professional growth as I navigated this transition.

The same goes for you. You don't have to walk your road alone. Your family and loved ones want you to be at your best. In addition to my immediate family, my brother and sister always supported me taking time off work for numerous personal and professional trainings, workshops, and retreats. My mother supported me with words of encouragement. My YPO forum and friends who ran businesses encouraged me to take the leap into coaching. Several of them hired me to work for their teams or referred me to leaders who needed an executive coach. I will remember those acts of kindness for life and it inspires you to help others starting a new business. You'll probably also be surprised how supportive those closest to you will be when they see you passionately following the purpose inside you.

A myth of self-actualization is that you have to leave everyone behind and become completely self-focused. That's not necessary or healthy. The reality is that you can't do life alone and you shouldn't have to. Aliveness is about becoming the best version of yourself not just for you but for those around you.

· · · · · · · · · · · ·

**Aliveness is about becoming the
best version of yourself not just for
you, but for those around you.**

· · · · · · · · · · · ·

It's about bringing your true self to those relationships. If you do that, I think you'll enjoy family and friends more than ever. While there will be rocky moments and hard conversations, if you're committed to being the best version of yourself, you will change, and people will notice. I believe you'll become a better spouse, a better parent, a better boss, a better friend, a better neighbor, and a better leader.

1. Think about the people on your team or in your company. Consider when you felt closest to them. What was happening? What words describe that feeling? How do you typically show them that you care about them?

2. How would you define love? How do you think love is shown in the workplace?

3. Do you think you have a mindset of love? How is that reflected in your life on a practical level?

4. When are you hardest on yourself? Do you ever struggle with seeing yourself as worthy of love or compassion? What would you tell your best friend, significant other, or child if they did the same thing?

We've looked at seven simple but powerful mindsets that together make up the Aliveness Mindset:

1. Ownership
2. Openness
3. Awareness
4. Authenticity
5. Courage
6. Tenacity
7. Love

These are ways of thinking that I come across regularly in leaders who are successfully pursuing an aliveness mindset. There are others, but these seven will carry you far on your aliveness journey.

Remember, you don't have to be an expert in every one of these to experience aliveness. It's less about achieving mastery and more about making progress. So if one of these areas resonated with you and you know you could improve, start with that one and see what happens.

> Looking at the seven mindsets, see if you can jot down personal stories that embody each one. Is there a trait you have a harder time thinking of an example?

Next, we're going to dive into the *practice* of aliveness. In other words, how do you become more alive each day? What are the practical things you can add, remove, or adjust in order to become more alive? Having an Aliveness Mindset is only the first step. It's what enables you to give yourself fully and authentically to the journey of discovery. But the real goal is to experience aliveness firsthand.

That's the goal of the next section: Aliveness Practice.

PART III

ALIVENESS PRACTICE

ALIVENESS IS SOMETHING YOU HAVE TO EXPERIENCE FOR YOURSELF, not something you simply learn about from a book. That's the point of this section, Aliveness Practice.

I want to show you how to define what aliveness means for you (chapter 13), break the experience of aliveness down into personalized key components called Anchoring Mindsets (chapter 14), and give you a number of practical suggestions and tools to experience aliveness on an ongoing basis (chapter 15).

Let's begin!

13

FEEL IT:
YOUR PERSONAL BRAND
OF ALIVENESS

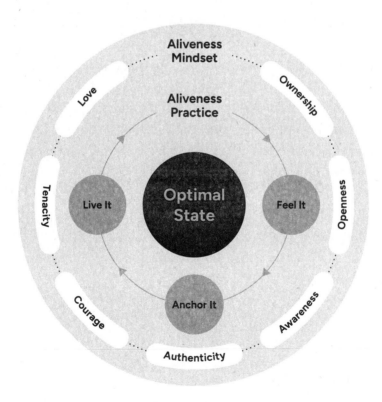

THE CIRCLE OF ALIVENESS WAS BORN OUT OF MY OWN EXPERIENCE, difficult as it was. It started with listening to a quiet, long-ignored voice within me, reminding me that there was more to life than closing deals and meeting payroll.

During my last few years as a CEO, while I was doing deep work on myself and learning how to be a more conscious, intentional leader, I realized that I had been orienting my days all wrong. I had been focusing entirely on efficiency, productivity, and progress. That was where I got my value and my sense of fulfillment, but it meant I was totally at the mercy of my calendar and to-do list. I was not leading. I was being led.

I thought I needed to check items off my list and keep busy "accomplishing things" in order to feel alive. Isn't that what living means? Doing things?

Of course not. It's *part* of living, but not all of it, and not even the most fulfilling part.

After nearly fifty years of "getting it done no matter what," it became abundantly clear that my focus on action and accomplishment, combined with my lifestyle of reacting to my schedule rather than choosing my schedule, was no longer working. I was burned out and unsatisfied. Even when we closed big deals, I felt none of the excitement and fulfillment that I expected to feel from accomplishing what I had set out to do.

I finally woke up and realized what I was doing to myself. I was killing my aliveness, not creating it.

Why? Because I had never slowed down long enough to define what being alive meant for *me*.

Did you catch that? For *me*. Not what it meant for my board. Or for my siblings. Or even for my idealized view of what a husband or father "should" do. I had never given myself permission to explore what Jack Craven needed, wanted, or was capable of.

Have you considered what aliveness feels like for *you*? Throughout this book, I've encouraged you to do just that, so I'm sure you've been thinking about it along the way. But we're going to dig deeper into that question right now. This is the heart and soul of the aliveness journey. You can't pursue what you can't define. You have to learn what aliveness feels like for you before you can understand how to align your life in such a way that aliveness becomes your daily experience rather than a few fleeting moments here and there.

I've shared so many stories of CEOs and business leaders because I want to emphasize just how personal this journey is. That is precisely where the power of aliveness is found: in its connection to you. To the deepest part of you. The subconscious part. The hidden part. The part that you might never have allowed to surface, the part that might even embarrass you a little, the part that can feel selfish when you engage it. At least at first.

In my case, the problem wasn't that I was working hard or chasing big goals. The problem is that I was expecting those things to make me alive, and I was sacrificing what *would* have made me alive in the pursuit of things that left me empty. Aliveness is within you, so aliveness must be defined by you.

. . . .

**Aliveness is within you, so aliveness
must be defined by you.**

. . . .

Nobody else can tell you how to be fulfilled. Nobody else can understand you better than yourself. So how do you find it? How do you define it? Let's explore that together.

Learning to Listen to Yourself

Learning about your aliveness starts with feeling it. Before you can define it, before you can analyze it, before you can create it—you have to feel it. You have to reconnect with the aliveness inside you on an emotional, intangible, heart level.

How do you feel it? I don't think there's a one-size-fits-all-approach to any of this, but I can tell you how I did it, and I can tell you how I work with my clients to get in touch with their feelings.

For me, it started with a reaction to a negative feeling. I felt dead. I felt frustrated. I felt angry. I felt resentful. I felt underappreciated. I felt so many negative things, and I came to the point where I had to ask myself, How do I *want* to feel?

I knew something needed to change. I wanted more out of life than just powering through my to-do list. Instead of feeling dull and uninspired, I wanted to feel more alive. I wanted to prioritize doing the things that I loved doing. I wanted to enjoy the journey, not just grit my teeth and try to retire with more toys than the next guy.

So here's what I did.

I listened to myself.

You might have expected something more dramatic, but this was really where it all started for me, and it's where it needs to start for you too.

I didn't go on a retreat to some remote Montana mountain. I didn't smoke mystery herbs with a shaman in South America. I didn't abandon everything I was doing and hole up in my house until the universe revealed its secrets. I simply focused on still-ness and listened. I turned my mind inward with intentionality, grit, and passion. I started listening to the voice inside me that was nudging me away from what was stealing my energy and toward what would recharge and reenergize me. I began paying close attention to my head, heart, and gut. What made me happy? What made me sad? What stole my passion? What got me excited? What did I want? What was I bored by? What did I do best?

Meanwhile, in my day-to-day responsibilities, I kept going. I was still a husband and father. I still had a business to run. There were bills to pay, decisions to make, and obligations to fulfill. I couldn't check out from my current life while I pursued aliveness.

This is important. Learning to listen to yourself is a process, so don't toss responsibility to the wind while you get in touch with the inner you. You can do both at the same time.

This is also why it's important to pursue aliveness now rather than waiting until you reach a breaking point. Proactively pushing forward into aliveness gives you space and margin to explore what your inner self is longing for while still continuing to function as a healthy leader.

Learning to listen to yourself means paying attention to the clues that your inner aliveness is giving you. It means noticing what works and what doesn't for your personality, your situation, and your life goals. Only you can understand your aliveness because only you can hear your heart speaking.

Your Personal Brand of Aliveness

In chapter 1, I asked you to attempt to begin to describe what aliveness felt like for you. We have walked through the components of an Aliveness Mindset, and you'll be able to understand better than ever what makes you feel most alive. You should be less resistant to questioning your status quo and more infused with faith and courage that you truly can build a life you enjoy living.

As you strive to connect with your personal "brand" of aliveness, as I like to think of it, focus on engaging the mindsets we looked at in the last section: ownership, openness, awareness, authenticity, courage, tenacity, and love. They will help you discover your aliveness and remain in that state.

If you remember our definition of aliveness, we said it is a state of being where you are *bringing the best version of yourself into your day-to-day experience through identifying and adopting mindsets and actions that align with your unique way of being fully alive.*

We'll get to the alignment part in the next two chapters, but for now, notice the last phrase: "your unique way of being fully alive." That's what we're looking for when we think about aliveness. We're trying to describe *your* distinctive aliveness experience.

So what is that unique version of aliveness? That's what you get to figure out.

I work on this concept with nearly every leader I coach. Not necessarily in the first session, because often there are mindset issues we need to work through first. But once someone is in a frame of mind where they are "all in" on their aliveness, I ask them to explore what being truly alive feels like to them.

The best way to answer that question is to remember specific times you felt alive. (Again, I referenced this in chapter 1, so some of this is review.) When have you felt in the flow, in the zone, lit up, on fire, unstoppable? When have time and space disappeared for you and you were fully immersed in the moment?

For example, in a recent coaching session, I asked Lyndsay, a senior executive with a software company in the Midwest, when she felt most alive. I gave her ten minutes to think of a few examples. As memories bubbled to the surface, she smiled and quickly scribbled different phrases down.

When Lyndsay finished writing, she shared her memories with me. First, she recalled the time her company landed their first big client. Then she mentioned an instance when she was on stage at an industry conference and was respected as a thought leader. She recalled the moment she thought of a new direction to take her company that applied cutting-edge technology. She smiled even bigger when she talked about reading a book to her daughter before bed.

Then, I asked her to attach a mental note to those memories that said, "This is when I felt fully alive."

How about you? I encourage you to take ten minutes and do this same exercise. Try to jot down three to five specific examples of moments you felt fully alive. These could be memories from your adult life, including your career, or they could be childhood memories.

Your mind, heart, and body remember those moments. Just relax and let them come forward. Summer camp memories...traveling across Europe...getting married...career victories...the birth of a child...practicing a hobby...completing a marathon... This is not about reaching for something outside yourself or creating something new. It's not about writing down what you "should" say. It is a process of focusing attention on the aliveness that is already there. Think back to moments that brought you deep joy, peace, excitement, and fulfillment. Don't just remember them in your head, but remember what your heart and body felt in those moments of aliveness. Where prompted by the questions below, write down what came up for you. What images came to mind? What words describe the essence of that state of being? Be as detailed as possible, but don't try to get it *right*. There is no right or wrong way to encapsulate your aliveness, because you cannot incorrectly describe yourself to yourself. Your description might be incomplete because you're still getting to know yourself, but it's not wrong. Silence the inner critic. This reflection on you at your best will be something you return to and continuously work with as you refine precisely what words describe you in your Optimal State.

The most important thing to remember is that this is about *you* and how you experience yourself at your best. Everything about this process begins and ends with you. Eventually others may help refine (not define) your self-reflection, but that will come later. Right now, the focus is solely on you as your own source of wisdom.

As human beings, most of us learn to take cues from others and our environment to determine how we should think, speak, and act. This is a natural process of seeking to belong in the environment we live in.[35] In fact, it is a key survival skill.

Learning to navigate the roles and expectations of those around you is an essential part of life, but if it is done without an established sense of self, the desire to "fit in" can supersede our own values, preferences, and needs. When fitting in becomes more important than authentic self-expression and self-fulfillment, we find ourselves waking up one day wondering, *How in the world did I get here?* We realize we weren't paying attention to what we have been creating, doing, or becoming.

That can be a startling and frightening realization. But it can also be the catalyst for your aliveness journey. When you realize that you have been existing unconsciously rather than living intentionally, it means that you are now consciously aware of yourself. That is where the journey begins. Set aside self-judgment and the need to fit in, and simply consider what makes you feel most alive.

1. Write down three to five specific memories where you felt most alive. Be as descriptive as possible about what you were doing and who you were with.

2. It's recommended that you share your aliveness memories with people close to you. Share each memory and speak about it as if it is happening in the present tense. Take about one minute per memory. Then ask them what traits or themes they notice about you in each memory. Their perspective can help you identify your traits of aliveness.

3. What words describe the feeling of aliveness to you? *Peace? Thrill? Buzz? Joy? Gratitude? In the zone?* See if you can come up with at least three terms or phrases that describe how you experience your aliveness.

4. Review the seven traits of aliveness (ownership, openness, awareness, authenticity, courage, tenacity, and love). Do you see these traits in your aliveness memories? If you can't see the seven traits in your memories, can you think of other memories where you can see the missing traits?

If you are having trouble remembering or describing your aliveness, you can take another route that utilizes your imagination. I often do this with clients as well. Everyone dreams of what things could be like if circumstances were different. So the pivot here is to shift from a *memory* of feeling aliveness to a *dream or imagination* of feeling more alive.

Dreams can evoke physical sensations and emotions just like an actual experience. Dreams are powerful motivators. Even if you have never let yourself dream before, start now. Think about what you would like to experience. If it makes you feel alive, just go with it. Let images arise as a stream of consciousness. This process does not have to be linear and the ideas may not be fully formed. That's okay.

Take the images and concepts that appear and write them down. Don't judge them prematurely. At this point, you just want to generate ideas. Quantity of ideas leads to quality of ideas.[36] Tap into the aliveness your dream world is reflecting by answering the following questions.

1. If you didn't have any limitations or concern for obligations, what would you like your life to look like? What
   would be different? How do you imagine you would feel?

2. What sensations do you feel when you imagine yourself at
   your best?

Remember, the point of these memories or dreams is not to say that this is what you "must" experience in order to be alive. The memories are in the past and can't be recreated, and the dreams are only possibilities that may or may not come true. Rather, the point of this exercise is to imagine yourself fully alive and then work backward to determine what "alive" feels like to you. You're looking for a description of a feeling, of an experience, because that feeling is what you are going to seek to carry into your day-to-day experience.

Once you have completed the exercises above, you should have a tentative list of words or phrases that approximate your unique feeling of aliveness. If you can, try to narrow them down to one or two key words.

For me, as I mentioned at the beginning of this book, aliveness typically feels *giddy*. That's the primary term I use to describe my Optimal State. Don't worry about naming your Optimal State. That's something you can explore down the road, and we'll get to it in a later chapter. At this point, your goal is simply to remember or imagine what aliveness means to you, then put words to those feelings.

I share my experience only to give you an idea how specific and colorful your description of yourself might be. Clients I've worked with have used words and phrases such as *confident*, *decisive, connected, engaged, calm, curious, joyful connection, inspiring, insightful, inspirational*, and *passion* in this stage as well as many others. These things may or may not turn out to be their Optimal State. That's not a big deal at this point. What matters is that they are tuning into themselves. They are listening and learning.

I should mention that when I first started exploring aliveness, I didn't think of the word *giddy*. I first thought of *play*. Play, to me, was a great descriptor for aliveness. I knew that didn't quite encompass my entire feeling of aliveness, but it was a solid start. I put it on the shelf and gave myself time for a better word to emerge.

One day, *giddy* popped into my head. I looked it up in the dictionary, and it means "excitement, almost to the point of disorientation." When I read the definition, I smiled, and my body tingled. I thought, *That's exactly how I feel when I'm truly alive. If I could feel giddy every day, how amazing would my life be?*

Being specific and descriptive matters here because your goal is to align your thinking and action in ways that maximize your aliveness. So if you can narrow your specific brand of aliveness down to a few words or phrases, you'll be able to quickly assess if you are approaching any given situation with your best self.

We're going to dive deeper into how to carry these words into your day-to-day experience, and I'm excited to get there. Relax. Enjoy the process. Be intentional about exploring your inner self, but don't stress out over it either. Let your subconscious help you see your aliveness more clearly.

These exercises are just the beginning of learning to become a witness to your aliveness. Only you can know you, and only you can listen to you. I believe there is a voice speaking to you, calling to you, encouraging you that there is more. It's the voice of aliveness, and if you listen to it, if you learn from it, you'll never go back.

14

LOCK IT IN: YOUR ANCHORING MINDSETS

JILL RUNS A SUCCESSFUL MARKETING COMPANY, BUT SHE WAS HAVING family issues unrelated to the workplace that were affecting her aliveness. Specifically, she felt that all her life, her father had tried to control her and had ignored her boundaries. These beliefs had become part of Jill's mindset. Whenever she saw her father, who was now eighty-two years old, she noticed the things that confirmed that mindset. As a result, when Jill visited her father, she was distant and reactive.

When Jill began working with me, she spent much of her time complaining about her father. After about fifteen minutes, I asked Jill, "Why do you allow him to control you?"

She was speechless. She hadn't considered that there could be another way to look at her situation. I then had Jill take responsibility for her reaction with her father and for permitting herself to enter reactivity. Jill began to smile as she recognized a shift happening in her lifelong perspective. It didn't make the challenge easy, but it was a solid step in the right direction.

I asked Jill if there was another, more positive interpretation of how her father acted. She couldn't think of one. So I asked her to close her eyes, take a breath, and open her heart. I asked, "What do you appreciate about your father?" Jill said she appreciated that he always supported her, was independent, took risks, and overcame a lot of adversity in his life.

Next, I had her think of a recent time that she felt her father was controlling. I asked her, "What did you imagine he was thinking and feeling at that moment?" She responded that her dad was likely scared.

I encouraged Jill to replace the label *controlling* with "He's scared and he cares." I could see Jill's body relax as she said the words.

Later, Jill told me her reactivity and defensiveness almost disappeared. Notice that all of our work was focused on her mindset, not her father's behavior. Jill's power to change her experience with her father and the version of herself that she brought to their relationship was within her. It was in her mindset.

Sometimes I encourage people to make this into a mental game. By that, I don't mean taking their problems lightly. I mean make mindset-shifting into a challenge. How good can you get at using your mind to create aliveness? If you have a negative judgment that causes you to get reactive, how could you change your interpretation? Can you assume positive intent? Can you engage compassion? Challenge yourself to find ways to reframe your perspective and shift away from reactivity and into aliveness.

· · · · · · · · · · · ·

Our mindset is so powerful *because it doesn't rely on anyone or anything. We are in full control of our experience and interpretation of events.*

· · · · · · · · · · · ·

We discussed mindsets in detail in chapter 5. I believe that our ability to control our mindset is the most powerful tool we have to impact our aliveness and how we show up in the world. Our mindset is so powerful *because it doesn't rely on anyone or anything. We are in full control of our experience and interpretation of events.*

Introducing Anchoring Mindsets

This brings me to one of the most important, practical, exciting parts of your aliveness journey: Anchoring Mindsets, or AMs. Your AMs are special mental models, values, or drivers that underlie your aliveness.

In the previous chapter, I asked you to come up with a tentative description of what aliveness *feels* like for you. That is the first step in your Aliveness Practice because until you know what aliveness feels like for you, you can't define it. And if you can't define it, you can't pursue it.

In this chapter, we will explore how aliveness is connected to your *thoughts.*

To clarify, Anchoring Mindsets are different from an Aliveness Mindset, despite the similarity in sound. We discussed the importance of having an Aliveness Mindset in part 1, and we talked about seven foundational mindsets that all of us need to adopt if we're going to make any progress in our aliveness journey.

Anchoring Mindsets, on the other hand, are highly personalized. They are mindsets that are *specific to you.* They are essential components of your value system and your inner motivations. When you identify them and learn to intentionally engage your AMs, they help move you toward aliveness, regardless of how difficult of a challenge you might be facing.

I use the word *anchoring* because the effect of these mindsets is to keep you grounded and stable in your aliveness, even when winds of fear and change blow. They are a stabilizing force, a source of strength and protection when life is difficult and aliveness seems hard to hold hold on to.

Let me give you my Anchoring Mindsets, by way of illustration:
- Play
- Connect
- Learn and grow
- Impact

Those four things, for me, describe the cognitive side of my aliveness. They are mental models. They are inner drivers that I can intentionally activate to help me access my aliveness. These things matter deeply to who I am on the inside, and when I engage any of them or all of them, they move me toward aliveness.

I didn't choose them—I just recognized them. I analyzed and observed myself, and I found that these are the common denominators that are typically at play when I feel most alive. Your Anchoring Mindsets will likely be different from mine. (See the chart below for some ideas.) Just as I said when we discussed feelings in the last chapter, there is no right or wrong here. You don't have to explain your words to anyone. The goal is to discover the mental models and drivers that move *you* toward *your* aliveness. This is intensely pragmatic and personal. It's about what works for you.

It's important to note that these are mindsets that help you achieve your aliveness one step at a time. Think of it like golf. Very few people ever get a hole in one. The goal with golf isn't to land the ball in the hole all the way from the tee box. That's not realistic. Instead, it's to get the ball closer and closer until you sink a putt.

To do that, you need different clubs. Your driver goes the farthest, and it can often get you halfway there. Your irons take care of the shots from the fairway onto the green. If you land in a sand trap, you have a sand wedge and hopefully a little luck to help you get out. And once you're on the green, you turn to your putter to get the ball into the hole. Then you go back to your cart and have a beer to celebrate.

In a sense, your AMs are like different clubs. They aren't the goal in themselves, but they are an integral part of getting you there. Depending on the situation, you'll turn to different Anchoring Mindsets.

The end goal is aliveness. It's the state of existence we're calling an Optimal State where you can bring your best self into every experience. But you don't just pop right into your OS when you roll out of bed in the morning. You don't coast through your day in your OS even when things are going wrong. That would be like expecting to hit a hole in one every time you tee off.

No, you have to work at aliveness. You have to make it a daily practice. You're going to wake up cranky sometimes. You're going to get stuck in rush hour traffic. You're going to get bad news at work. You're going to deal with unforeseen challenges. In those moments, your AMs are the tools you pull out of your bag to knock the ball a little closer toward aliveness.

For me, *play*, *connect*, *learn and grow*, and *impact* are effective mental models. They are the clubs I know I can use to get me closer to aliveness because they work for me. They feel good in my hands. I know how to leverage them. They improve my game, guarantee progress, and contribute to my success in the pursuit of aliveness.

I'm going to walk you through the process of finding your AMs. Once you do, I think you'll quickly see their value. You'll be able to point to the practical things that underpin your aliveness. When you find yourself in a sand trap of reactivity, you'll know which mindset to reach for to move you closer to your aliveness goal.

First, take a look at the following list of common AMs. If any of them resonate strongly with you, circle them. Be open to other words. Really, the sky's the limit here. Or maybe I should say that the dictionary is the limit. There is a never-ending variety of descriptors that could anchor you to aliveness.

Once you skim through the list, read on to discover five questions that will help you define your Anchoring Mindsets.

Common Anchoring Mindsets

Abundant	Adventurous	Authentic
Buzzing	Calm	Carefree
Compassionate	Confident	Connected
Conquering	Courageous	Creative
Curious	Daring	Empathetic
Extroverted	Faith	Fulfilled
Funny	Grateful	Honest
Impactful	Informative	Joyful
Laughing	Leading	Learning and Growing
Openhearted	Play	Present
Relaxed	Serenity	Spacious
Still	Supportive	Surrendering
Thrilling	Trusting	Unflappable

Discovering Your Anchoring Mindsets

So how do you identify these mindsets that are so important to you? Just as with the feeling of aliveness that we discussed in the last chapter, you discover your AMs by looking inward and paying attention to what is inside you already. This is not a quick process or a linear one, so don't expect to come up with a perfect list in two minutes, and be open to refining or changing the list over time. Earlier I listed my four AMs, but I am well aware that there could be more to discover or that those could shift and change over time.

Below are three questions to help you explore and name your Anchoring Mindsets. Remember, you're looking for things that anchor you to aliveness, but it might take a little digging and a lot of thought, so be patient.

1. What elements are common to my memories of aliveness?

Look back over your list of memories from the last chapter. Are there specific values or drivers that stand out? Are there common denominators? Patterns?

Work backward from the feelings of aliveness. Deconstruct them. What were the underlying reasons that those memories felt so right to you? What were your thoughts at that time? What were you pursuing, valuing, or achieving that sparked your aliveness?

Maybe you notice that in all or most of the experiences, you felt deep joy, or peace, or relaxation. Those common denominators might be your Anchoring Mindsets.

2. What thoughts calm me, energize me, or otherwise move me toward aliveness?

Here, you are focusing not on memories but on your current way of dealing with different kinds of situations. How do you talk yourself through challenging moments? How do you calm yourself down? How do you bring stability to your thoughts and emotions? Try to identify what your coping strategies tell you about yourself. Your body and mind know a lot about self-healing and self-protection, and if you pay attention, you can learn a lot about what you truly need.

The things you naturally turn to for stability and energy might be indicators of what aliveness feels like for you. For example, if you have a potentially stressful meeting ahead, and you tell yourself, "I can do this," that might indicate that to you, aliveness includes a mindset of *confidence*. Or, if you recharge after a hard day at work by texting a friend to go out for drinks, aliveness for you might include *connection*.

3. What do I naturally feel, do, and prioritize when I don't feel threatened?

In other words, when you are not in a state of reactivity, how do you naturally behave? What do you seek? How do you organize your priorities? How do you use your time? You are looking here for clues to what your inner aliveness automatically does when it is free to act. It might be helpful to look again at your list of memories and notice what you gravitated toward during those moments of aliveness.

If you are overseeing a project that you feel excited about and capable of handling, and you don't have impossible budgetary or timeline constraints, how do you feel? If you are *creative*, or *bold*, or *trusted*, or *grateful*, notice that. Those things probably point to what the most alive version of you would look and feel like, which could indicate your AMs.

Also, pay attention to how you act when you are free to be yourself. For example, if you find yourself naturally drawing in multiple team members and empowering others, aliveness for you might have an element of *connection*, *mentoring*, or *generosity*.

4. What is sabotaging my aliveness, and how do I try to counteract that?

This is essentially the opposite of the previous question. What situations steal your energy or joy, and why? Think for a moment about that, then try to determine the antidote. Here, you're intentionally noticing your weaknesses or your tendencies toward reactivity, not to condemn yourself but to see if you can identify the opposite of those things.

When you have a time-sensitive, complicated project to finish and tensions are high, are you tempted to lock up? Lash out? Blame-shift? Give up? Feel guilty? These negative reactions can help point to what aliveness looks like for you, if you dig deep into what feels threatened and what you are trying to protect.

5. What do other people say about me when they are praising me?

We tend to spend a lot of time fixating on people's criticism, trying to deny, defend, or fix whatever is triggering their displeasure. Instead of that, I'm asking you to remember the compliments. What do people say you are good at? What impresses them about you? Don't focus so much on your talents, although it can include that, but on your values and character. Often other people can see what is important to us more clearly than we do.

I seek out feedback nearly daily from others around me. What was most impactful and why? What could have been improved? I regularly hear that people value my sincerity and stability. I can sometimes hear that I could tone down my intensity. Without feedback, I wouldn't see my blind spots or identify traits that others value that I now see as valuable.

Please note, this is not your starting point for self-definition. It should simply be confirmation of what you've already noticed or clues to value something about yourself that you've never thought was that special. Also, I'm not talking about what people say you "should" do or "could" do. Sometimes obligation and potential can be misleading.

If people often appreciate how open you are to new things, your experience of aliveness might include curiosity. If they notice how positive you are, maybe your aliveness includes mindsets like joy or optimism.

These five questions are the foundation of your aliveness mindset. Once you begin focusing on the mindsets that make you tick, you'll pick up on patterns—both good and bad—that you can then address.

The last thing to cover is how to use your Anchoring Mindsets. The goal isn't just to know more about what makes you tick. It's to use that knowledge to enter into aliveness. This is an Aliveness *Practice*.

Let me give you a personal example of how practical AMs are. As I've mentioned already, I am a perfectionist. When I am leading a team, I tend to believe that there is a perfect agenda, a perfect way to facilitate the team, and a perfect outcome to meetings. There is a cost to this mindset, though. I can be far too serious. I can carry too much pressure due to my self-imposed expectations. I can stifle creativity, limit my time, and in general be a poor leader out of a misguided attempt to get everything exactly right.

After a lot of self-reflection and helpful feedback, I came to realize that I am not at my best when I believe there is a perfect way to do things that I have to find. Armed with that awareness, it was up to me to change the way I think. I could say, "Hey, I'm just a perfectionist. Sorry, but you'll get used to it." But why would I identify myself with something that is undermining who I really want to be?

This is where AMs really shine. At some point, I realized that *play* is one of my AMs. It might even be the most important one because it's so closely linked to *giddy*. It's pretty much impossible to have a playful mindset and a perfectionist one at the same time. So *play* is a great tool to get me out of unhealthy perfectionism. My brain is wired for negativity, but by engaging play, I can hack the game to improve my odds of feeling alive.

Often before a meeting, I will say the words *play* and *giddy* to myself. I always write "PLAY" at the top of my training session outline in capital letters. I can never remind myself too often of that mindset. I will imagine myself with the team relaxed, smiling, and feeling playful. I visualize people engaged and laughing. When I do this, my body relaxes, a weight is lifted, and I show up at my best.

A play mindset always propels me into my OS. Why? Because if I approach what I am doing—meeting a client in a coaching session, working with a team on a challenge, being with my family—from a place of play,

- I am more curious and open to learning.
- I have more fun, and my team does too.
- I am more open to experimentation and risk-taking.
- I treat obstacles like a game to be won or a puzzle to be solved.
- I trust my instincts more.
- I cause others to have more fun because enthusiasm is contagious.

Do you see how practical AMs can be? They are your secret weapon. They are your way to hack the game. I could give a similar list for my other three AMs. They are truly powerful tools to anchor you to aliveness.

I don't expect you to have *play* as an AM, although maybe that's a great one for you too. (Wouldn't the business world be better if we obsessed less and played more?) Instead, I want you to discover your own Anchoring Mindsets.

Once you do, using them is simple. When you find yourself in reactivity, or when you are in a situation where your energy is being drained, think about your AMs. Say them out loud, if you can. Then make a conscious choice to approach your situation from those mindsets.

You might not be able to use all of them, but even one will get you closer to your Optimal State. For example, if I were attending a funeral, *play* would certainly not be the best way for me to bring my full self into such a solemn occasion. But another of my AMs, *connect*, is perfect. If I think of that word, it reminds me that even in such a difficult situation, I have something to offer. And for me, that is a direct pathway to aliveness.

This is more powerful than you might expect, as you'll discover when you try it. Just a quick moment of reflection, a simple redirection of your thoughts and focus, can make all the difference in getting the ball closer to the hole. What we tell ourselves often becomes our reality. Remember David Robson's book *The Expectation Effect*? "What we feel and think will determine what we experience, which will in turn influence what we feel and what we think, in a never-ending cycle."[37]

· · · · · · · · · · · ·

What we tell ourselves often becomes our reality.

· · · · · · · · · · · ·

Dive into this exercise with all your heart. I promise you, it's worth it. This is where I see clients come alive the most. It's a tangible, practical way to move yourself toward aliveness. Let the following questions guide you, then spend the next week trying them on for size. When you're in a difficult situation or when you simply feel low on energy, say these words to yourself and approach life through these mindsets.

If any of them don't resonate in the real world, toss them out. If they do, hold on to them, and see if you need to refine them further. Usually you'll end up with three to five unique words that will feel deeply personal to you.

Congratulations! You've just taken a huge step forward into aliveness.

1. What elements are common to my memories of aliveness?

2. What thoughts calm me, energize me, or otherwise move me toward aliveness?

3. How do I act when I don't feel threatened?

4. What is sabotaging my aliveness, and how can I counteract that?

5. What do other people say about me when they are praising me?

6. Based on the above questions, can you identify three to five Anchoring Mindsets? List them below, think about them during the week, then come back and make edits as needed until you are satisfied with them.

- _____

- _____

- _____

- _____

- _____

(15)

LIVE IT:
ALIGNED WITH ALIVENESS

TAKE SIXTY SECONDS AND GLANCE OVER YOUR CALENDAR. NOTICE what you have scheduled today, tomorrow, and the rest of the week, and pay attention to your visceral, gut-level reaction as you see each upcoming meeting or event you have scheduled. I encourage you to try this now, before you continue reading.

What did you feel? Which commitments increased your energy? Which ones diminished it?

Be aware that within a matter of seconds, your mind will attempt to figure out your energy and convince you of the validity of what you "have" to do. There is a place for that. Sometimes you have to go to difficult meetings or handle painful situations. But for the purpose of this exercise, we're concerned with your initial, visceral reaction. Often that is a more accurate reflection of how you feel about something. Your head can easily get clouded by emotions, obligations, and the duty of being a good leader, parent, or friend. Reflect on what you felt. How much of your calendar is determined by obligation? How many things in your day and week drain your energy? Is it just a few things here and there, or is the bulk of your time structured around things that don't contribute to your aliveness, and may even be sabotaging it? How much of your day *brings* you energy? What are you prioritizing?

Many of us lead a reactive life based on our calendar and schedule. That is, we go into our day and week scrambling just to take care of what slides across our desk. We check off tasks, take calls, hold meetings, and respond to emails, and we mostly are just trying to keep our heads above water.

This reactive way of life is considered normal in business, especially if you are a high-performing leader. This lifestyle has been modeled for us, demanded of us, trained into us. It's often held up as something to be celebrated, as if martyrdom were the mark of a good leader. The net result is leaders often invest a lot of time into things that drain their energy.

The ways this plays out are as varied as they are damaging:

- Leaders often feel obligated to attend meetings they've been invited to. They go because they don't want to disappoint the person who invited them, even if they have no real value add.
- Leaders are included in numerous nonessential emails about project updates or other noncritical topics that fill up their inbox and distract them from what they need to focus on.
- Leaders frequently get involved in unnecessary projects because a report of theirs is underperforming, but rather than communicate expectations better or make difficult changes, they shoulder more of the project.
- Leaders can easily busy themselves with projects that are in their comfort zone, rather than in the high-value area where they should be working, because it feels safer.

I'm sure you could add to that list, especially when you evaluate the things on your calendar this week that give you negative energy. These energy-draining activities are more than just a waste of time or physical energy. They are often directly correlated to your aliveness or lack of it. Why? Because if you spend the bulk of your time putting out fires, mopping up other people's messes, and wading through busy work, you're essentially existing in a place of reactivity. You are a prisoner to your calendar and other people's expectations. You aren't deciding how your day will feel. Your day is deciding how *you* will feel.

There is another way to live. You can be focused and intentional, making life happen in a way that places you in your genius zone and in the flow. To do that, you have to learn how to align your actions with what creates aliveness for you.

Prioritize How You Want to Feel, Not What You Want to Do

Look at our definition of a state of aliveness again: *bringing the best version of yourself into your day-to-day experience through identifying and adopting mindsets and actions that align with your unique way of being fully alive.* That last phrase summarizes the Aliveness Practice: *identifying and adopting mindsets and actions that align with your unique way of being fully alive.*

Notice the words *mindsets, actions,* and *align* in that definition. In the last chapter, we talked about mindsets. We called them Anchoring Mindsets, and we saw the value in identifying specific ways of thinking that effectively move you back into aliveness.

In this chapter, I want to talk about actively aligning yourself with your aliveness. I want you to ask yourself, "What can I do to feel more alive? How can I structure my commitments, conversations, and calendar to reflect my aliveness rather than resisting or suppressing it?"

If you are like most leaders, much of your life revolves around what others need, want, or expect rather than on what you want to create. As I said before, that is what is expected of you. "The buck stops here," the saying goes, which we take to mean that we are ultimately responsible if anything is left undone. There is always more to do, which means that what you really *want* to do either doesn't get done or only gets the leftover crumbs of your time and energy.

So what's the answer? How can you go from dreaming about aliveness or talking about aliveness to actually *living it*? Let me share something that has helped me tremendously over the years.

As I've mentioned, I spent multiple years as a stressed-out CEO. Then I began a coaching practice—and promptly became a stressed-out coach! Sure, I was more excited and less frustrated than before, and I was finding incredible personal satisfaction in my work, but I soon realized that I had imported some of my bad habits and unproductive mindsets into my new career. I had subconsciously begun to reproduce the same frenzied, high-pressure, expectation-driven lifestyle that had eaten me up as a leader.

It was easy to justify. There was definitely an urgent need to make money, attract clients, and build a business. Plus, my perfectionist nature naturally creates a performance-driven value system. Between the needs around me and the drive within me, I was once again descending intro reactivity.

After a few months of this, Judy started making some gentle but pointed comments about my work schedule. Thanks to the years of working on myself, I was a lot quicker at taking constructive criticism than before. Plus, the last thing I wanted was to recreate the toxic work environment I had paid such a high price to leave behind. After a lot of self-analysis, I finally realized that I needed to prioritize my aliveness over my accomplishments. I needed to make sure that my actions were congruent with my distinctive way of feeling alive rather than in competition with it.

The key to aligning your day-to-day experience with your inner aliveness is to *prioritize how you want to feel, not what you want to do*. That means every day, you look at your schedule through the lens of how you want to feel throughout the day.

· · · · · · · · · · ·

The key to aligning your day-to-day experience with your inner aliveness is to *prioritize how you want to feel, not what you want to do.*

· · · · · · · · · · ·

This is a critical mindset shift you must make too. It runs counter to the hyper-efficiency teaching most of us grew up with, but it leads to greater sustainability, satisfaction—and, ironically, efficiency.

I'm not talking about being controlled by your feelings. If you've achieved any success in life, you've learned the value of self-discipline and delayed gratification. Often you must do the right things first, even when they are hard to do. The good feelings come later. I'm not contradicting any of that—I'm a big fan of work ethic, integrity, discipline, and responsibility.

The problem, is that in the name of "work ethic" and "self-discipline" we can end up denying, suppressing, postponing, and ultimately betraying the true desires of our hearts. When I say prioritize how you want to feel, not what you want to get done, I'm talking about paying close attention to those deep, lasting longings of the heart. I'm talking about your need for satisfaction, contentment, gratitude, love, connection, and peace. I'm talking about a sense that your life matters and your work is making a difference. I'm talking about leaving a legacy you can be proud of.

Building a successful company, earning millions of dollars, or being featured in magazines is great, but at the end of your life, is that what you want to be known for? Is that what you want to give yourself to? Is the price you have to pay to attain those things worth the quality of life you have to sacrifice along the way?

I'm not saying your goals are wrong (that's for you to decide), but I am encouraging you to continually evaluate the philosophies and mindsets that guide your journey. I'm trying to nudge you toward prioritizing your experience of aliveness (intrinsic value) over your accomplishments (extrinsic value) for the rest of your life.

Prioritizing your feelings or your experience of aliveness implies two things at the same time. They are the two sides of the alignment coin. First, choose to carry aliveness into your day. Second, choose to structure your day to support your aliveness. Let's look at each of these in more detail.

1. Choose to Carry Aliveness into Your Day

This means changing how you think: your mindsets, your expectations, your inner dialogue. This is the mental choice to bring the best version of yourself into your day. This is where your Anchoring Mindsets really shine, because they enable you to shift your attitude and approach out of reactivity and into aliveness, even when you're doing things that aren't particularly exciting or easy. They help you not only do them but do them authentically, from a place of aliveness, which transforms the entire experience into something that increases your energy rather than draining it.

After you make this priority switch, you will still do a lot of the same action items as before, including some difficult, disagreeable ones; but the way you *think* about them should change. Instead of coming from a place of "I have to get this done, so I'm going to get it over with as fast as possible and move on to the next thing on my list," you can operate from a place of, "I choose to engage in this activity. I'm going to align my mind and actions with aliveness to the best of my ability. I'm going to savor the process, even if it's not always easy; and I'm going to celebrate the result, even if it's not perfect."

2. Choose to Structure Your Day to Support Aliveness

This means changing what you do on a practical level: *ruthlessly* restructuring your calendar, choosing what meetings to be at, having conversations with people whose underperformance is draining your energy or who need to perform at a higher level, and so on.

This actually isn't complicated. When you prioritize how you want to feel, you naturally make lifestyle choices that expand and amplify your feeling of aliveness. However, on a practical level, I've seen many leaders resist these first steps because it often requires candid conversations that might disappoint others on your team. I recommend that leaders give context when having these conversations, explaining that these changes are in service to everyone having more impact and being more energized and productive.

Most of my clients have had the same action-oriented patterns that I used to have. As I work with them to prioritize their heart and gut, not just their head, they often express that they wish they would have thought this way years ago. It's not that they hate their jobs but rather that they have allowed the demands of the job and the world around them to lock them into a lifestyle that is out of alignment with who they really are. Once they identify their own flavor of aliveness and they commit to making that their priority, they begin to get clarity on how to align their calendars, to-do lists, meetings, and decisions in such a way that they can bring their best, full self into all they do.

With practice, you'll learn when you need to choose to lean into the power of your mind to reframe your experience in a particular situation versus when you need to take steps to adjust the situation itself. Just remember that both are important. You can't demand the entire world change to make you more alive, but you also can't gaslight yourself into thinking you are the problem and you just have to grin and bear it.

This starts with a choice and it's yours.

You have to prioritize feeling alive over getting things done.

You'll still get things done. But you have to put one of these things above the other, and most of us prioritize doing over feeling. I'm inviting you to flip the script. Start with how you want to feel, then work backward from there. I think you'll be surprised how much clarity it brings in your daily schedule.

Let me stress here that making these changes is not about being defensive or self-protective. Those are reactive states, while the changes I'm describing are about opening yourself up. They are about growing, learning, expanding, and becoming who you really are. Don't frame this as "I can't do this anymore" or "I'm getting burned out" or "The stress is too much for me." Those things might be true, but they are symptoms of something, not root causes. They indicate a lack of aliveness, and the cure is to become more alive.

So when you decline meetings, delegate responsibilities, or hold your reports to the standards they should have been meeting all along, you aren't failing or abdicating your role. You are becoming a better leader and a bigger person. Don't let people around you or the voice inside you frame these changes as reactivity—it's *proactivity*, and it's *authenticity*, and it's *courage*.

Productivity Is the By-product, Aliveness Is the Goal

Interestingly, this shift in perspective toward starting with how I want to feel and leaving space to savor the experience has not negatively impacted my productivity or my efficiency. If anything, it has improved it while also improving my quality of life along the way.

I've seen the same thing happen with my clients, and I believe you will experience it as well. When you carry the right mindsets into your job, you tend to do things more efficiently and more effectively. When you choose how you want your day to feel, it's easier to identify things that are threatening your aliveness—such as meetings that could have been emails, and emails that could have gone to someone else. This filtering process contributes to your productivity and your aliveness at the same time.

The point cannot be first and foremost productivity. That's just a by-product. Focus on experience. This is your life, and you get to live it only once. When you choose how you want to feel about each day, *you are effectively choosing how you want to feel about your life.* The significance of that cannot be overstated.

Since I made the switch years ago and reoriented the way I approach my day, I experience life more fully. I focus more on savoring the moment (although I still miss some). I enjoy the fruits of my labor rather than just checking off tasks on my to-do list. I look for moments throughout the day to feel alive. I've gone from a task-oriented way of moving through life—where I was always hurrying, always busy, always behind schedule—to one in which I truly experience life. I focus more on enjoying anticipation rather than just completing or getting through something. I see myself as capable of more than I ever did before, and I envision greater things for my future. I attract and invite different types of people into my world. I am doing things that I never thought I'd be doing. I welcome new people and new perspectives, and that expands my world.

Yes, I'm a work in progress. But I'm enjoying the work, and I'm celebrating my progress. And it feels so damn good that I want everyone else to experience it too.

Alignment is a process. You don't need to achieve total alignment by next Monday morning, and attempting to do so would likely do more harm than good.

Instead, take one step today, then take another tomorrow. That step might be to adjust your inner world so that you take a better version of yourself into your day, or it might be to cancel something on your calendar because you know it's not what you need to be doing with your time and energy. Every step forward is a choice, and it's a choice for your aliveness.

Remember, you'll have to keep learning how to create alignment because life changes, and so do you. You'll never outgrow the need to listen to yourself. You'll never get your calendar perfectly structured. That's okay. The point is aliveness, and aliveness is dynamic, not static.

That is why it's important to celebrate your successes along the way. We often are so focused on what we lack or the next goal that we forget the progress we've made on our journey.

Use the following questions to help you visualize the kind of day and the kind of life you want to lead. Then make whatever choices you need to—internal and external—to create a life of aliveness.

---

1. If you haven't done this already, scan your upcoming schedule and evaluate your energy. On a scale of 1–10, how alive does your current schedule make you feel? Based on your scheduled time commitments, how well does your calendar align with your priorities in life? Are there specific meetings or responsibilities that you have a negative visceral reaction to? What do you think your inner aliveness might be telling you? What do you want to add or prioritize in your calendar?

2. How do you want to feel today? This is probably similar to the words you use to describe your aliveness. It might include your Anchoring Mindsets. Write down a short description of how you want to feel throughout the day.

---

3. What specific, tangible things could you change to structure your life for greater aliveness?

Like other parts of the aliveness journey, this isn't a onetime exercise.

You'll need to follow the cycle we've discussed in this section again and again. *Feel* your aliveness, which means learning to describe how you personally experience it. Then *anchor* yourself to aliveness by engaging your unique Anchoring Mindsets as often as you can, in whatever situation you need them. And finally, *live* this all out by intentionally aligning your lifestyle in a way that creates more aliveness. Then, start over. Feel it again, but with more clarity. Anchor it with more understanding and skill. Live it out with greater efficiency and in new areas. And so on, ad infinitum. That's the Aliveness Practice.

In the next section, Optimal State, we will explore a number of practical tools to not only get aligned but stay aligned. I'm excited to share them with you because I've seen how these principles and strategies have helped countless people, and I believe they will do the same for you.

Can you envision a life where you have autonomy over your daily experience? Where you are able to decide how you want to feel? Where aliveness is more than a nice idea or theory, but it becomes a description of your lived experience?

It's there—you just have to choose it, step into it, and begin to grow in it. It simply takes practice. Aliveness Practice.

PART IV

OPTIMAL STATE

LIVING IN YOUR OPTIMAL STATE IS ABOUT BRINGING THE BEST, MOST alive version of you into your daily life.

That starts with an *Aliveness Mindset*, which we covered in the first section. You have chosen to own your aliveness, to be open and aware, to be authentic to yourself, to be courageous and tenacious, and to love. You've set your mind to this. You chose yourself.

Then, you learned about *identifying and adopting mindsets and actions that align with your unique way of being fully alive,* which is the essence of the *Aliveness Practice* we discussed in the previous section. Now that you've identified the mindsets that anchor you to your specific brand of aliveness, you will become more skilled at aligning yourself to what creates aliveness for you.

With a little practice, you can find yourself *bringing the best version of yourself into your day-to-day experience.* That's the essence of this section: your *Optimal State.*

It's not just about feeling like the best version of you once in a while, or when conditions are perfect, but about bringing that "best you" into every facet of your experience.

I've already said so much about the Optimal State that you probably have a good handle on what it is, and you might even know what word or words describe your Optimal State. I want to cover specific areas that often come up in client conversations.

One common question is this: How do you know what your Optimal State is? We'll cover this in chapter 16.

Second, how do you stay in your Optimal State? Life has a lot of...well, shitty moments. We'll talk about this in chapter 17, where we'll discuss one of my favorite metaphors: the Castle of Aliveness.

And finally, what are some strategies to move from reactivity to aliveness? We'll explore a list of practical, effective Living All In tools in chapter 18.

16

HOW DO I KNOW?

JONATHAN WAS THE CEO OF A HOSPITALITY COMPANY THAT WAS pursuing outside venture capital investment. The economy wasn't doing well at the time, so Jonathan was pleasantly surprised at the level of interest. He had more offers than he expected, and the VCs were considering investing significant capital.

You would think he would be excited. Instead, when we spoke, he was stressed out and overwhelmed at all the work he and his team needed to do to respond to the due diligence documents: everything from financials to HR reports.

I asked him, "Can you tell me what you are most focused on?"

He said, "All the work we have to do."

"What if you switched the focus of your attention from the work ahead to the excitement of an outside investor paying a premium for a portion of the business?"

That simple question made an obvious difference in his demeanor. Of course he was excited—he just hadn't let himself *feel* excited because of the urgent matters at hand.

I asked him to envision this opportunity as a jelly-filled doughnut. I told him to imagine taking a huge bite of the doughnut and having jelly all over his smiling face. That image totally changed the way he related to the experience.

How we relate to the experience *is* the experience.

That's the whole point of the Circle of Aliveness. Throughout these chapters, we've discussed aliveness not as a goal to achieve someday but as an experience that you can step into at any moment and grow into as you go along. Another way of looking at this is that aliveness is not the finish line at the end of the race.

It's the race itself.

I'm starting with that reminder because I know how high-functioning leaders think. I work with business leaders every day, and I am one. I'm all too familiar with an efficiency mindset that says, "Just tell me what I need to know and what I need to do. I'll get that done, check it off, and move on."

But with aliveness, and in particular with your Optimal State, there is no box to check. The moment you turn your aliveness into a to-do item, you undermine the whole thing.

Your aliveness is *you*. And you are not a box to check off.

This is the reason I left the center of the Aliveness Circle for the end of the book rather than starting with it. Your Optimal State is not something you can name, define, and perfect in a fifteen-minute exercise. As a matter of fact, in my work with clients, I rarely spend much time on their OS at first. Some of them never define their OS, and that's fine.

Optimal State is, by definition, hard to define. It's a *state* of aliveness, which means you're describing the ongoing condition of experiencing feelings that are uniquely important to you. It should be pretty obvious that reducing something so subjective to a word or two might not be a straightforward process. However, the more clearly you are able to discern and define your OS, the more motivated you will be to reach it.

The terms matter less than the experience. As I've mentioned, my OS is *giddy* because giddy is how I typically experience aliveness. When I am spending significant time in a state of giddiness—which for me is excitement, flow, high energy, even physical tingling—that is my Optimal State. But at some point, I might realize that there is a better word than *giddy*. Or, as my life continues, my experience of aliveness might shift, and I could end up describing my OS differently.

I'm really not stressing out about this, and neither should you. If the terms help, use them. If they get in the way, toss them. If, by the end of this chapter, you can name your OS, that's wonderful. But if, by the end of this chapter, you can't name it but *you're getting better at living in it*, that's a thousand times better. This book will have succeeded in its goal. Many clients call one of their Anchoring Mindsets their OS.

Describe what aliveness feels like to you as specifically and concisely as possible, because that will help you assess yourself and pinpoint areas that need change. Name your Anchoring Mindsets, or most of them at least, because those are concrete ways to align your day-to-day life with your inner aliveness. But even those things are a work in progress since you never stop changing.

Like Jonathan, I want to invite you to focus on the experience of life because *that is life.* And with that important clarification out of the way, let's take a closer look at Optimal State.

Understanding Your Optimal State

I'm going to share five brief observations about your Optimal State, which is the goal of the Circle of Aliveness. I've discussed most of these at one point or another, so some of this will be review, but I think it will be helpful to see it all in one place. As you are exploring what it means to you to live in your OS, please remember:

1. Optimal State is an experience, not an action.

Have you ever been to a scenic overlook, a concert, or a family event, and you were more obsessed with getting a good picture than experiencing what was happening? Maybe your spouse or friend finally grabbed your arm and said, "Just enjoy the moment."

That's what your OS is like. Being in the moment. Noticing, feeling, taking in with your senses everything that is happening. This is the reason I call it a state. It's how you exist, not just how you act.

You can feel intensely alive when you are not doing anything at all. You can feel intensely alive while you're doing something difficult or uncomfortable. Aliveness is within you, as I've said before, and your Optimal State is about experiencing it regardless of outward circumstances.

Of course, aliveness usually leads to positive actions. When you are in your OS, you'll often be wonderfully productive. We'll discuss "flow" later. But when it comes to your OS, you must *live in it* before you can *live it out*. If you skip the feeling and jump right into doing, you've missed the heart of the matter.

2. Optimal State is your personal brand of aliveness.

We've discussed the individualized nature of aliveness at length, so I'll just remind you that your OS is about you. Nobody else can define it, judge it, control it, or predict it.

In a way, the title of this chapter could be misleading. When you read "How Do I Know?" you might have expected me to give you a list of surefire steps to define your OS. In reality, that question is aimed at you.

How do *you* know?

You know something. It's deep within you. What do you know now? What do you need to know? How could you know yourself better?

It is in answering those questions for yourself that you will discover your aliveness.

3. Optimal State is you at your best.

It's not you living somebody else's best. It is not you fulfilling everyone's expectations and demands. It's not you living out some idealized image you might have had of yourself.

It's about uncovering (or discovering) you at your *true* best. It's you aligning your mindsets and actions with who you really are so that you can *live fully* and bring *your full self* to life.

"At your best" is a value statement. It's why you should take your OS seriously. And it's not just best for you, either, but also best for others. You need to be you, and people around you need you to be your authentic best self. Don't limit yourself because you have martyr syndrome or a savior complex. Be the best *you* possible, both for you and for those who depend on you.

4. Optimal State is a place you spend a lot of time.

That's the goal. At first, it might be a sporadic experience. But with practice, you'll learn to have more access into your OS. And if you find yourself in a state of reactivity instead of your OS, you'll recognize what is happening and take steps to get closer to your OS.

This is a game of seconds. Every second you are not reactive is a second you can feel alive.

· · · · · · · · · · ·

This is a game of seconds. Every second you are not reactive is a second you can feel alive.

· · · · · · · · · · ·

It goes back to the daily choice I mentioned earlier. When you prioritize how to experience each day, you are choosing how to experience your life. We all want to get to the end of our lives and be able to say we lived fully, with no regrets. The best way to make that happen is through a daily habit of living in, or as close as possible to, the center of your aliveness.

5. Optimal State is not always possible, but you can always move closer to it.
We aren't talking about some happily-ever-after state of nirvana, heaven, or euphoria. We're talking about life, and life is not exactly easy at times. So don't expect to be in a state of permanent bliss.

But don't settle for too little either. Don't resign yourself to trudging through your day, barely surviving. Remember the golf club metaphor? Maybe you can't hit a hole in one and feel fully alive right now, but you can make a move in the right direction.

Whether you find it helpful to sum up your Optimal State in one word, two words, a phrase, or even a picture, the main point here is that it's *yours*. You own it. You value it. You're committed to it. You are getting better at feeling it, anchoring it, and living it.

The more you do this, the more aliveness you experience. You begin to be more *yourself*, more *often*, in more *ways*, at more *times*. That's the ongoing and always-growing result of investing in your aliveness. It changes you and it changes how you show up in the world.

Flowing in Aliveness

Earlier, I mentioned that aliveness is a feeling that leads to actions, not the actions in themselves. How you experience something *is* the experience. How you live *is* life.

That doesn't mean that aliveness is inactive or ineffective. I've stressed throughout this book that I believe the opposite is true. When you are truly alive, you'll bring the best version of yourself into whatever you do. When you are in your OS, you are more focused, more creative, more energized, and more effective than ever.

Psychologists and researchers use the phrases "in the flow" or "state of flow" to describe a similar experience. The concept of flow was popularized by a psychologist whose name I can never pronounce but whose ideas resonate deeply with my experience: Mihaly Csikszentmihalyi. His book *Flow: The Psychology of Optimal Experience*, explores this concept in detail.[38] Others have built on his work since then, and today it's an important leadership and business concept.

Flow is a psychological state of complete absorption and focus on an activity. Distractions fade away, and you have a sense of clarity and natural concentration. When you are in the flow, it's common to lose track of time. Because you are so caught up in your experience of the moment, you often transcend all sense of time, and hours can feel like minutes. You are performing at optimal capacity. While the activity requires work, the work feels almost effortless; and while it might be challenging, you know you are enough for the challenge. So rather than feeling bored or overwhelmed, you feel inspired. The activity draws on your special skills, values, and interests. It brings out the best in you.

Flow is often connected to a sense of control over your actions and a belief in your ability to overcome obstacles. This autonomy and self-efficacy give you a sense of empowerment and increase your motivation. As a result of bringing your best self to the task at hand, you often feel a deep sense of fulfillment and enjoyment.[39]

As I've mentioned, my OS is *giddy*, and it shares a lot of similarities with the flow I've just described. For you, flow might feel peaceful, or powerful, or emotional, or energizing, or all of the above. The point isn't so much to define it as to experience it.

And to do that, you have to get in touch with your aliveness. I've seen time and time again that optimal *performance* is a natural by-product of being in your Optimal *State*. Being a high-per-forming leader is not about forcing yourself to live a life you hate; it's about learning to adjust your own mindsets to view your life differently *and* about discovering what naturally brings out the best in you.

How about you? Can you think of times where time stood still, the world around you faded away, and the energy to face a challenge came from within?

Don't assume those moments are the exception. They should be the norm. Make a habit of bringing the optimal version of yourself into your day-to-day experiences. Don't settle for "it's not that bad" or anything else that is less than the best you.

1. How would you describe your Optimal State? Be as specific and concise as you can.

2. Describe a time you were "in the flow." What were you doing? Why do you think it was so captivating for you? What can you learn about your aliveness from this experience?

3. Look at your calendar for today. Choose one task, then write down two or three practical ways you could do that task from your Optimal State. What mindset do you need to carry into it? Is there anything you need to change about it? What is within your power to do that will enable you to bring the best version of yourself into that task?

$$\left(\;17\;\right)$$

ALIVENESS IS THE RULE,
NOT THE EXCEPTION

I REMEMBER ATTENDING A YPO FORUM IN EARLY 2013, BACK WHEN I was deep in the process of wrestling with all the mindsets we've looked at in this book. I was trying to express to the group how dissatisfied I felt with my life. One of the forum members responded by asking me, "Is it that bad?"

I froze. On paper, my life wasn't that bad. It was good, actually. I had a lot to be happy for. I was CEO of a stressful but successful business, and I had a strong marriage, three wonderful daughters, and a solid income. That's a great life, right? Or at least, it's not a bad life. What else could I expect?

But something clicked inside me at that moment. I realized "It's not that bad" wasn't the metric I wanted to live my life by. *He lived a life that wasn't that bad* wasn't the epitaph I wanted carved on my gravestone.

For twenty years, my career had been defined by "It's not that bad." Now, I was ready to raise the bar. A lot. I didn't want to live a "not that bad" life with a few moments of genuine aliveness sprinkled in. I wanted to flip the script. I wanted aliveness to be the rule, not the exception. I wanted to feel energized and passionate. I wanted my life to count.

This concept of staying in aliveness is one that I want you to envision for your own life. Your Optimal State is not just a goal to strive for; it's a place to stay. To live *in* and live *from*. And if you do stray from this place of aliveness for whatever reason (which we all do), you should try to return as soon as possible.

When working with clients, I often ask them to think of something tangible to represent what "staying in their OS" or "feeling alive" means to them. For me, I envision being in a castle, and that metaphor is an easy way to remind myself that my goal is a lifestyle of aliveness. I want to stay in aliveness, not just visit it.

Take a minute to think about what place or object could represent staying in your OS. Maybe there's a real place that could provide a visual connection for you, such as the beach, a forest trail, or a cabin where you always vacation; or maybe a different metaphor comes to mind. I'm going to use the castle metaphor to illustrate a few important practices relating to aliveness, but feel free to substitute your own place of aliveness.

I want you to imagine being in that place of aliveness. In *your* aliveness. Your personal brand and definition of what it means to be truly alive. It's your castle. You design it. It's perfect for you. When you are in your castle, you are in your OS. You are in charge. You are safe. Protected. Happy.

This metaphor emphasizes two things: a feeling of aliveness that is unique to you, and the fact that you want to spend as much of your time as possible in this place, which represents a life spent primarily in your OS.

Note that the castle is not your circumstances but rather your *experience* of those circumstances, as we saw in the last chapter. So when I say, "You are in charge," I don't mean you rule the outside world with an iron fist and everything always goes your way. I mean you rule your *inner* world. When you are in your castle, you are in control of your thoughts, your words, your time, your feelings. You are in your Optimal State. You are fully alive, and you are bringing your best self into your day-to-day experiences.

Sometimes, for whatever reason, you'll find yourself at a distance from your castle, from your OS. You won't always experience complete alignment with your aliveness. You definitely won't have warm, fuzzy feelings all the time. But you do need to plan to go back, which is where your Anchoring Mindsets come in. Regardless of how far away you have to go, as soon as you can, begin to return. Move a little closer. Don't give up until you cross the drawbridge and sit back down on your throne.

The castle metaphor (or whatever other metaphor you choose) should remind you to make this feeling your home base, rather than reactivity. In my experience, when I leave my OS, it's because I've switched from aliveness to reactivity. Reactivity is essentially the opposite of an Optimal State because you are no longer in control of your environment. You are a prisoner of it. Unconsciously, you can chain yourself to reactivity and feel powerless to change.

While it's normal for that to happen once in a while, how long you stay there is up to you. You have the power to return to your castle anytime you choose. I'm not saying it's easy to get back to the castle if you've left it. I'm saying *it is always possible*, and I'm saying *the choice is yours*. As queen or king of your castle, you must embrace those two essential principles.

In order to leave reactivity behind and return to your OS, you'll often need to deal with some things that are getting in the way. Let's examine a few of the common blocks to aliveness.

Removing Aliveness Blocks

Since your aliveness is distinctive to you, your blocks are as well. You have your own kryptonite, your own Achilles' heel. We all do. These blocks keep you out of your Castle of Aliveness.

If you pay attention to your feelings throughout your day-to-day experiences, you will generally be able to pick up on the situations or triggers that most affect you. This is a matter of awareness and wisdom. Once you identify your blocks, you have multiple tools at your disposal to minimize reactivity. It's the unseen obstacles that trip you up, not the known ones.

Here are some common blocks I have found in my experience and conversations. This is just a starting point: feel free to add to the list if you have experienced additional blocks.

Addictions	Ambiguity or uncertainty	Anger
Boredom	Distractions	Ego or self-righteousness
Entitlement	Exhaustion	Family conflicts
Fear	Feeling attacked	Feeling disrespected
Feeling out of control	Feeling overwhelmed	Feeling threatened
Feeling underappreciated	Hunger	Ignorance
Irresponsibility of others	Laziness	Loneliness
Mistakes or failure	Negativity	Need to be right
Obligation	Overscheduling	Past traumas
Perfectionism	Pessimism	Seeking approval
Self-doubt	Shame or guilt	Social interaction
Stress	Suspicion	Underperforming leaders

Notice that some of these are internal and some are external. Many of them are not necessarily bad, and most of them are unavoidable at times. You're not trying to eliminate every possible pain point from your life. You're just looking for the triggers that tend to affect *you* the most so that you can address them and get back to your castle.

Another way to better understand why you are getting reactive is to reflect on whether a core need (approval, control, security) is being threatened. Understanding the perceived threat can help you begin to question it.

I remember working with Sarah, the founder of a successful B2B software company. Sarah recognized that she was more concerned with being liked than feeling alive. Because of this, she often avoided having difficult conversations with underperforming leaders on her executive team about areas where they were falling short. When she did try addressing the issues, she often diluted her message out of concern for how she might be perceived or out of fear that her feedback would demotivate them. The cost was that her team did not know when Sarah was disappointed or where they fell short.

I acknowledged how admirable it was that Sarah cared about the people on her team and didn't want to be too critical. I asked her what was causing her reactivity and blocking her aliveness. She reflected then said, "I'm feeling overwhelmed and judging my team as underperforming." I'm concerned that if I give them critical feedback they will be deflated and also not like me."

I reminded her of her Anchoring Mindsets: warmth, confidence, and being present. I then challenged her to consider the cost of holding back constructive feedback: she often worked late in order to correct what her team produced as it did not meet the clients' expectations. Another longer-term cost was that she was not getting the most out of her team and she was getting involved where it was her team's responsibility.

We took small steps. She paused and took a few breaths to slow down and get present. I then asked her to imagine her team rising to the challenge and her being a mentor. What would a mentor do?

Sarah said that she will create a list of which reports were under-performing and what each needed to do differently. I then had her draft a review for each of them that started with, "You'd be an even better leader if..." By framing the feedback with these words, she felt more confident and was less concerned that the leaders will be deflated and not like her. It also allowed her to exhibit warmth, another of her Anchoring Mindsets. We then role-played conversations for each underperformer.

I like to have my clients open their conversations with a "head-line." Headlines tell the other person right away the direction of the conversation. I don't think it's effective for the person who is receiving feedback to wonder, *Where is this conversation going?* When your headline is, "I'd like us to discuss that I was disappointed with your proposal and how you communicated with the client last week," there is a mutual understanding of the topic of the conversation. In role-plays, I always play the underperforming leader and give my clients feedback on their tone, the clarity of messaging, and how well they were able to create a tight plan for next steps.

After our role-playing session, Sarah felt more confident and clear on conversations she needed to have with several members on her team. Within a month, she had the courage to commit to all of the conversations she had been avoiding. As a result, the reports on her executive team had a better understanding of where they had to level up. They committed to a plan to improve, and they had metrics for both sides to measure the progress. Their work quality became measurably better. Sarah didn't have to work late as often because her reports were stepping up, so she had more energy and greater impact. Not only that, her commitment to her aliveness meant she modeled for her team the importance of speaking candidly when there were issues. Her team experienced her as a leader who helped them grow, and they witnessed her feeling alive.

Like Sarah, only you can identify what is blocking your aliveness. It might not be the same thing that would block someone else. It may take some trial and error, but make a commitment to identifying and addressing your blocks.

When you read through the list above, did any of them stand out to you? Or can you think of something that is not on the list? Be honest with yourself. Be vulnerable and humble. There's a lot of freedom in that. The purpose of identifying obstacles is gaining awareness and returning to aliveness, not judging or condemning yourself for who you are.

If you are a high-functioning leader, you might be used to hiding your weaknesses, but part of aliveness is embracing them. Obviously I'm not talking about excusing behavior that is harmful toward others. I'm talking about being honest with your humanity. What you call "weakness" might not be weakness at all. It's just who you are, and you are not weak.

By nonjudgmentally recognizing when something triggers your reactivity, you remove much of its power to control you. You give yourself permission to make needed changes. That might mean taking a thirty-minute break after a meeting to get back into your OS. It might mean scheduling difficult calls in the morning while you're fresh. It might mean blocking out times in your schedule where you cannot be interrupted so you can focus on being creative. It might mean hiring someone to do the things that deplete too much of your energy. It might mean having direct and candid conversations in the moment they are needed.

The forest outside the castle is not a bad place to visit, but don't set up camp there. You have a castle to get back to. You might find yourself lost in reactivity from time to time, but don't stay stuck there feeling helpless. Remind yourself that leaving your castle is a choice, and so is returning to it. Cross the drawbridge or climb the stairs, then return to your OS.

Nothing should stand in your way.

Accelerants

We just looked at one important practice to remain in your OS: *removing blocks*. Let's look at one more before we close. I call this one *accelerants*. Accelerants are small, practical actions that help you activate, sustain, extend, and maximize your aliveness.

I realize the concept of *accelerants* may not fit the medieval castle metaphor very well, but I use the term with my clients, so I'm going to stick with that.

Accelerants are things that connect you to yourself in a way that brings clarity to your mind and energy to your body. They activate alignment between the *doing* part of you and the *being* part of you. Here are some examples.

Being in nature	Biking	Breathing
Cultural events or museums	Dancing	Daydreaming
Doing nothing; unstructured time to think	Drawing or painting	Exercise
Family	Friends	Generosity
Hobbies	Journaling	Laughter
Listening to a podcast	Meditating	Music
Reading	Solitude	Sports
Taking a bath	Taking a class	Vacation
Walking	Watching a movie	Yoga

I'm sure you could add a few to that list. Just as with blocks, accelerants are very personal. There are probably some things on this list that sound stressful to you that would relax me, and vice versa.

Becoming aware of your accelerants is an immediately effective way to keep yourself in a state of aliveness or to begin the return trip to your castle if you've left it and gotten a little lost. These are actionable, schedulable things that you can turn to at any time.

We tend to call these "me time" or "self-care," or we say things like, "This helps me recharge." They *are* a form of self-care, but my hesitancy with terms like that is they sound a little defensive. To me, accelerants are more than just feel-good routines that help you cope with the stress of life. They are powerful, proactive tools that propel you toward your OS and keep you in your OS longer.

Instead of looking at them as survival techniques or coping mechanisms, view them as intentional steps toward the aliveness you deserve. When you view accelerants this way, they become strategies at your disposal that you can employ at any time. Rather than waiting until you are mentally or emotionally fried, plan ahead. Schedule a few of these things into your day.

One word of caution: don't confuse adrenaline with aliveness. In particular, be careful of engaging in risk-taking activities to "feel more alive."

I'm not talking about blowing off steam by participating in adrenaline-inducing activities such as dirt-bike racing or skydiving. If that's your thing, great. Nor am I talking about engaging in risky behavior, including illegal or unethical activity, as a toxic way of handling an overly high stress level. Something that makes you "feel" alive in the moment but actually sabotages what really matters to you is not a good thing. Adrenaline is a short-term survival chemical produced by your body. It's not a long-term plan for energy, and it can lead to burnout and stress.

Genuine accelerants do the opposite. They allow you to handle pressure in a healthy way so that you don't end up hurting yourself or someone else, and they move you toward the kind of person you want to be, and the life you want to have, over the long haul.

For me, cycling is one of my primary accelerants to spur creativity and build confidence. I've learned how to leverage that. When I'm riding my bike, my mind is an open slate. Typically, the first part of the ride is letting go. I debrief the day in my head, make a mental note of any follow-ups or insights, and then wipe the slate clean. Once my head is clear, I bring clients or concepts into my consciousness. I allow thoughts to flow and ideas to come from my intuition or gut feelings. Once an idea begins to form, I notice my excitement and continue following the path of creating more excitement. Those ideas tend to be bold and edgy. I look for ideas that make me feel giddy. I'm not concerned at this point whether a client will like the idea or not. That comes later. I'm just creating. I record all of my thoughts into my phone, and I can generate ten to thirty ideas per one-hour ride.

Cycling isn't the only accelerant that I rely on. I vary my accelerants intentionally each week. Sometimes it's walking in nature, other times it might be blocking out time and listening to music. The goal is for me to be focused on what will help me get into my OS. I am committed to making accelerants a priority in my daily routine because of the positive impact they have.

Creativity is just one of many areas that accelerants can facilitate. Maybe you need confidence. Maybe you need peace. Maybe you need wisdom. Maybe you need courage, or rest, or healing, or joy. Rather than waiting until the needle hits zero, fill up your tank in advance. Schedule an accelerant before or after a challenging appointment.

Find what works for you, then invest in yourself. You don't have to justify your accelerants to anyone else. If you enjoy knitting, knit. If astronomy is your thing, buy a telescope. Don't judge yourself.

Be like a child in this regard. Kids don't second-guess what they want to do, and often they are more in touch with their aliveness than most adults. Pay attention to what you like to do. If it increases your energy, helps your mood, sparks your creativity, and heals your soul...don't you think it deserves to be prioritized?

Your Aliveness is yours, but no one is going to force you to take the throne. That's up to you.

Are you up for it? Are you willing to stay in your OS as long as you can? Are you committed to removing blocks that get in your way and to finding ways to return to your castle when you stray?

If so, congratulations, I believe you've got a lot to look forward to. Nobody can guarantee that it will be easy, and life is certain to throw you a few curveballs. But when you learn how to bring your unique brand of aliveness into your day-to-day experience, nothing can keep you from making the most of life.

---

1. What percentage of your time would you say you currently spend in your OS? Out fighting battles? Stuck in the reactivity?

2. Look at the list of blocks again. Can you identify three to five blocks, either from this list or your own experience, that tend to affect you the most? Keep these in mind when we cover tools to reduce reactivity in chapter 18.

3. Review the list of accelerants. What are three to five activities, either from this list or your own experience, that usually lift your mood or otherwise restore your aliveness? Which one(s) could you do today? Would you be willing to make accelerants a priority nearly every day?

18

LIVING ALL IN (LAI) TOOLS

IF YOU DON'T HAVE A PLAN FOR WHEN YOU GET REACTIVE, IT'S NEARLY impossible to minimize reactivity in the moment. That's why it's critical to have not only an awareness of *patterns* that make you reactive but *tools* at your disposal to counteract the reactivity.

The fifteen LAI (Living All In) tools I'm about to unfold are tips and strategies I use with my clients to help them discover and remain in their Optimal State. The more tools you have, the more likely you'll spend a greater amount of time in your OS. Experience is the best teacher. If some of these are a little harder than others at first, give it some time. And if you find that some work better than others for you, use those! The best tools are the ones you'll use.

I mentioned earlier that I didn't make these tools up. I've collected them over the years, and I've refined them for my own practice in some cases, but you can find extensive information about nearly all of them online, if you are interested in learning more. For the purposes of this book, I'm going to give a brief overview and show how these tools can serve you in your aliveness journey.

That said, this chapter is lengthy, so I encourage you to read through and then come back to the tools that resonate most with you in your experience. The tools are not in a specific order. Again, feel free to skim them, apply them, adapt them, or add to them as you see fit.

1. Identify reactivity

This is more than a tool: minimizing or neutralizing reactivity is one of the key concepts of aliveness, which is why I've discussed it in detail throughout this book. The goal is to be *aware* sooner when you are reactive, use a tool of your choice, and return to your OS.

One of the best tools for awareness is from *Start Here: Master the Lifelong Habit of Wellbeing.* Just remember these three words: *Notice. Shift. Rewire. Notice* reminds you to become aware of where your attention is directed. Are you present or distracted? *Shift* redirects your attention to the present moment. *Rewire* reminds you to take fifteen to thirty seconds to savor your experience and reinforce the shift you just made.[40] I love the simplicity and the impact of this concept. Using this tool can help you create new, healthier patterns.

Suggestions for using this tool

a. Learn to recognize what reactivity feels like for you in your body. Tension in your shoulders? Shallow breathing? Stomach pain?

b. Learn to recognize how you manifest it. Freezing up? Lashing out? Making rash decisions?

c. Ask others how they experience you when you are reactive. This can be an eye-opener when it comes to identifying your blind spots.

d. When you start to feel reactive, breathe until you settle down a little.

e. Name the specific situation or story that you are telling yourself that triggered the reactivity. It's often your interpretation of events that is creating much of the reactivity. Instead of saying, "My team doesn't care. They don't appreciate me. They didn't give their best effort," is there another, more positive way to frame what happened? For example, "My team did their best, and there are areas they can improve."

f. Finally, analyze what core needs are being threatened. Approval? Control? Security?

You may use other LAI tools in conjunction with this process, but the process itself is therapeutic. Often by the time you get to the root of your reactivity, you will have already left that negative state and begun to restore aliveness.

2. Identify resistance

If you've ever done yoga, it's likely that you learned to spend the first couple of minutes just feeling your body, noticing where there is resistance or pain. This is a nonjudgmental process of not only becoming aware of areas that might be suffering but also respecting those sensations and listening to what they have to tell you.

The same goes for resistance in your emotions or thoughts. Spend time noticing where and how you are resisting things in your life. I don't just mean resisting positive change either. I mean resisting your current situation as well.

The point here is not to judge yourself or even fix yourself. It's certainly not to force yourself to do something you aren't ready for. Instead, it's to listen and learn. The places where you are self-protecting deserve kindness and care. Just as you wouldn't force your legs into a lotus position if you weren't that flexible, you shouldn't try to force your soul into a position it's not ready for.

I often ask clients, "Are you resisting something that is reality?" I'm not saying that they should *want* that thing to happen, but they need to recognize anything they are subconsciously denying. Sometimes I'll even ask people to stand up and push against the wall to demonstrate the futility of resisting something that already exists.

As with identifying reactivity, identifying resistance is often therapeutic in and of itself.

Suggestions for using this tool

    a. Learn to recognize how you tend to manifest resistance. Defensiveness? Blame-shifting? Busyness? Refusing to give in? Denial? Do you take out your anger on others? Clam up? Hunker down in your private bunker and withdraw?

    b. Check in with yourself and notice if you are resisting anything. This could include accepting circumstances, accepting your limitations, or accepting the need to change, among other things.

    c. Try to identify any fears underlying your resistance. For example, fear of not being enough, fear of being rejected, fear of not finding a solution, fear of letting people down.

    d. Show yourself compassion (see also tool 5) and employ positive self-talk (tool 9). Speak kindly to yourself and try to defuse those fears.

    e. Finally, do your best to accept whatever you have been resisting. Acknowledge its existence and simply let it be. You can work on solving it later. Just sit with it until it loses its power to intimidate you.

3. Breathing

Deep breathing and relaxation practices activate the parasympathetic nervous system, which tells the anxious part of your brain that you're safe and don't need to remain in a fight, flight, freeze, or fawn state. It also carries more oxygen to the brain, which aids in reasoning.

There are numerous breathing techniques available for you to try, and I encourage you to explore what works best for you. Most of the techniques I've seen employ belly breathing, or breathing from the diaphragm, and that is what I generally recommend.

Suggestions for using this tool

a. When you realize you are getting into a reactive state, stop what you're doing and sit still.

b. Breath from your diaphragm, slowly, focusing on your breath. I often recommend Dr. Andrew Weil's 4-7-8 breathing technique to reduce stress and blood pressure.[41] It's simple and addictive (in a good way). Whenever I am feeling stress—such as when I'm at the airport or late for a meeting—I use this technique. Inhale for a count of 4, hold your breath for a count of 7, and exhale for a count of 8. Do that cycle four times. It helps!

c. Repeat for a couple of minutes or until you feel ready to use diagnostic tools, such as exploring your reactivity or resistance.

4. Meditating

As with breathing, there are many excellent resources available for meditation practices. I encourage clients to incorporate at least a five-minute meditation practice into their daily routine. This is more for maintenance, though, so if you are in a particularly challenging time, or even if you just had a stressful day, a few extra minutes can do a lot of good.

Suggestions for using this tool

a. Find a time and place where you can fully relax.
b. If you don't have your own meditation practice, it can be helpful to search "guided meditations" on Spotify, YouTube, or another platform of your choice. My favorite is an app by Sam Harris called *Waking Up*.
c. Pay attention to your breathing: slow, deep, belly breaths.
d. See what works for you! There is no right or wrong way to do this.

5. Self-compassion

Author and scholar Kristin Neff describes self-compassion as our attitude toward ourselves during moments of perceived failure, inadequacy, or personal suffering.[42] It involves not only quieting our inner critic but also embracing compassion and concern for our own distress. Neff emphasizes that practicing self-compassion means we are mindful of the pain or mistakes we are going through, but we are not overly identified with those things. We might stumble or fail in specific instances, but we are not failures as individuals.

She also highlights the importance of recognizing our shared humanity. As humans, we all experience suffering and imperfections—it's a natural aspect of our existence. By understanding that we are not alone in facing difficult situations, we can foster self-compassion more easily.[43] Humanizing our difficulties empowers us to confront them. Daniel Pink, when discussing Neff's work in his book *The Power of Regret*, states, "By normalizing negative experiences we neutralize them."[44] He goes on to reference research and studies in which individuals with self-compassion proved to be more adept at managing regret[45] and showed higher levels of optimism, wisdom, curiosity, and happiness.[46] Self-compassion helps people take accountability and address their challenges in ways that lead to positive transformation.[47]

Self-compassion is a tool most of us should use a lot more. For high-functioning leaders, this can be a challenge because you're used to going, doing, pushing, challenging, profiting, planning, buying, selling, and most of all *winning*. But what happens when you come face-to-face with your limitations? Do you spiral into shame? Blame yourself for not being good enough? Demand perfection even though it's impossible?

Many of us are better at showing grace to other people than we are to ourselves. We give them second and third chances, we believe the best about them, we work with them to overcome weaknesses, we encourage them along the way—and then we give the person in the mirror absolute hell for every little mistake. That doesn't seem healthy, does it?

In particular, don't be too harsh on a past version of you. Yes, admit your mistakes and hold yourself accountable. But you can't expect that version of you to know what you know now, or to be who you are today. Every iteration of you deserves compassion.

Suggestions for using this tool

   a. Acknowledge the limitation, weakness, or mistake with humility and honesty.
   b. Silence your inner critic. Shut them down and shut them up. This is not the moment for critiquing or analyzing.
   c. Speak to yourself as you would a friend or family member if they were in your place. Would you encourage that person? Console them? Defend them? Support them? Do the same for yourself.

d. Finally, contemplate the future with compassion. You might be facing a challenge, but you don't have to be perfect. You don't have to get it right the first time. Give yourself permission to be less than perfect.

6. Self-distancing

Self-distancing describes a variety of cognitive techniques that create psychological distance from your own thoughts, emotions, or experiences. The goal is to mentally step back from a situation and observe it from a more objective standpoint in order to gain perspective, regulate emotions, and make wiser decisions.

Daniel Pink explains self-distancing as a method to gain perspective on our experiences, enabling us to analyze and strategize objectively. He compares it to shifting our role from a scuba diver submerged in regret to an oceanographer, piloting above the water to observe its shape and shoreline.[48]

As with many of these tools, there are many ways to do this, and I encourage you to find what works for you. In my practice, I do several different things. I'll share three of them below.

Suggestion for using this tool

a. One technique is *self-coaching*. I will often ask clients to tell me what they would tell someone else who is going through a similar situation. This can include encouragement and emotional support as well as practical advice.

b. Another technique is verbally separating yourself from your emotions. For example, instead of saying "I am angry," say "I am *feeling* angry." This is not just semantics. In the first phrase, you are simply living the emotion. In the second, you are identifying the experience as a feeling and giving yourself permission to experience it. But don't stop there. Say, "I am *aware* that I am feeling angry." In this

stage, you are reminding yourself that you exist inde-
pendently of the emotion and have autonomy over it.

c. A third technique is to feel your emotions all the way
through. First, name all the feelings you are experiencing.
Check for any form of anger, sadness, or fear. Then, locate
these in your body, breathe deeply, and quietly ask yourself,
"Can I allow the sensations to be there for ninety seconds?"
More often than not, the sensation will dissipate.

7. Rehearsing OS and AMs

I use this tool all the time: I ask my clients to repeat their Optimal
State (OS) and/or their Anchoring Mindsets (AMs) out loud. Most of
the time this simple act is a solid step toward returning to their OS.

Of course, you first have to have a fairly good handle on what
your OS and AMs are. Once you do, put them to use by referring
to them regularly, especially when you're facing something that in
the past would have triggered reactivity.

I encourage clients to put pictures on their desk or computer
background that represent their OS and AMs. For example, I have
photos of me with my family and our dog, Riley, that represent
play. I have another photo of Judy and me that represents *connect*.

Suggestions for using this tool

a. When you feel reactive, say your OS and/or your AMs aloud.
b. Take a few seconds to evaluate whether you are operating
in your OS. If not, can you change something? Specifically,
would one of your AMs help you move one step closer to
your OS?
c. Decide whether you need to adjust something in you (your
mindset) or whether you need to make a specific change in
your calendar or leadership to create alignment.

8. Accelerants

See chapter 17 for an in-depth discussion of accelerants. Remember, these are things that help you return to aliveness. They are things that work for you, specifically. If you need a mindset shift or a mood reset, this is often the place to start.

Keep in mind that an accelerant is not a toxic coping mechanism or a cover-up for something that needs to be addressed. It's an action that is healthy for your body, soul, mind, or emotions.

Suggestions for using this tool

a. Identify what your accelerants are. You probably already know some of them because you've naturally gravitated to them throughout your life. Be open to trying new things.

b. Identify when they are most effective. Maybe you are most creative when you are in nature, or more efficient when you have jazz music playing in the background. I have a list of songs on my Spotify playlist that reliably elevate my mood. One of my go-to songs that makes me happy is listening to "Sister Golden Hair" by America. I can't explain it, but hearing that song works every time! For many people, different accelerants work at different times and for different situations.

c. Build them into your schedule proactively. Don't wait until you are burned out. Instead, take initiative to plan healing, energizing activities into your day. Take advantage of the push they give you.

d. Don't be afraid to call a time-out in your day and turn to one of your accelerants, even if you hadn't planned on it. It might just be two minutes of meditation or a brisk walk around the building, but give yourself permission to reset when needed.

9. Inner coach

Most of us have an inner critic, but I suggest you fire them and hire an inner coach. Listen to the voice in your head that encourages you, not the one that belittles or criticizes you.

If you don't have a voice like that in your head, then *be* the voice. Give yourself regular pep talks. Affirm to yourself that you are capable, you are good, you are qualified, and you are the person for the job. This is not just hype or self-deception. Psychology consistently affirms the importance of positive self-talk.

The hardest part is silencing the inner critic that society and culture have instilled in our heads. You have to be brutal about this because it's so easy to say things like, "I'm so inconsiderate," "I'm such an idiot," "I can't believe I made that mistake." That's not you speaking: that's your inner critic. It's just using first-person pronouns to fool you.

Author and entrepreneur Tim Ferriss interviewed performance psychologist Dr. Jim Loehr. This is how Loehr coaches his clients on their inner critic: "The power broker in your life is the voice that no one ever hears. How well you revisit the tone and content of your private voice is what determines the quality of your life. It is the master storyteller, and the stories we tell ourselves are our reality."[49] I'm struck by the fact that *how* we talk to ourselves has one of the biggest impacts on our happiness. Once again, we control our reality and our experience.

Psychologists sometimes refer to automatic negative thoughts, or ANTs. These are spontaneous and often distorted or negative patterns of thinking that arise automatically and unconsciously in our minds. They include catastrophizing, excessive self-blame, overgeneralizing, all-or-nothing thinking, assuming the worst about others' opinions of us, and accepting our negative emotions as if they were reality.

Don't just ignore your ANTs: use them against themselves. For example, if they are pointing out weaknesses, change the negative statements to affirmations of growth. One of my clients who wasn't good at public speaking changed the negative thought "I'm not good at public speaking" to "I'm not good at public speaking *yet.*" Another client changed the same critique to "I'm on my way to improving my public speaking."

As I mentioned above, it can be helpful to talk to yourself as if you were someone else. What would you tell your child if they were in your shoes? Or a friend? Or someone on your team?

Suggestions for using this tool

a. Learn to recognize the voice of your inner critic. Intentionally silence that voice and refuse to believe its assessment of you. If you need help separating the critic from yourself, ask a loved one what they wish you would quit believing or saying about yourself.

b. Learn to recognize your particular ANTs. Then, consider how you might hack the ANT and use it to your benefit by changing the things you think and speak about yourself to reflect growth.

c. Proactively speak affirming words. For example: *I can do this. I am good at this. I am qualified. I am loved. I always find a way. I know how to do this. This is going to work.*

10. Reframing

Reframing refers to changing your perspective about something so that you view it in a more favorable, hopeful light. This is not self-deception or mind games: it's choosing to challenge any default, fear-skewed mindsets and replace them with positive mindsets. It's believing the best about yourself, other people, and circumstances around you.

Much of our reactivity stems from the stories we tell ourselves and the judgments we pass. Both of these are interpretations, meaning that another person can have a different interpretation of the same event. We connect the dots based on what we see and experience to create a narrative—often a negative one—about people or circumstances. Then we believe that *our* interpretation is an accurate reflection of reality.

Reframing occurs when we use our awareness of our reactivity pattern to create thoughts and phrases that reduce the sense of threat. We do this by becoming aware that it is our interpretation of events that is causing us to become reactive, not the events themselves.

When we are in reactivity, our focus gets all "effed" up: we fixate on *fear*, *fault*, and *failure*. When we return to our OS and engage a positive, productive reframe, we focus on what can be learned, what can be done, and what comes next. That's a much better way to live.

I often ask my clients to share situations that are "third rail" reactivity triggers. By that I mean specific situations that have always been so highly charged for them—like the third rail in electric train systems—that they typically get very reactive, very quickly. I help them see how the ability to reframe can neutralize even third rail reactivity situations. That is power.

I was working with a team once that was in the process of launching a new product, and several issues negatively impacted the launch. Teams were blaming each other for the miss: "Sales didn't execute the plan" or "The marketing team didn't have a great strategy." I began the team meeting by having everyone acknowledge their disappointment that the results fell short. I had the teams appreciate the efforts of all involved. Then I asked everyone to close their eyes and think of their Anchoring Mindsets or OS.

Finally, I shared a quote by James Clear to help them reframe the situation and take responsibility: "Without altering the facts of the situation I am facing and without ignoring the reality of what must be done, what is the most useful and empowering story I can tell myself about what is happening and what I need to do next?"[50] Instead of blaming one another, the teams began sharing all that they'd learned from this "failure" and what they would do differently. The atmosphere shifted immediately.

Reframing is a great tool to use when we find ourselves speaking words that block or impair our aliveness. Kate ran her own venture capital fund. She was very proud to have a diverse leadership team, a strong mission, and a clear focus on the types of investments they made. When I heard her talk about her fund, I noticed she used the word *small* a few times. As we talked further, I gleaned how she saw her fund in comparison to others. It impacted her confidence, her executive presence with her team, and how she presented herself externally. I gave her feedback on how that one word impacted so much, and she removed it from her lexicon. The change in how she viewed herself and interacted with others was dramatic. Within a year, the size of the fund tripled due to her focus and efforts.

The reframe is also a good tool to use when you become reactive based on someone else's behavior. I invite clients to become curious when someone else gets triggered. Stephen Covey says, "We judge ourselves by our intentions and others by their behavior,"[51] and reframing attempts to turn that around. Ask yourself, *I wonder what just happened to explain why they are behaving that way?* When we practice this reframe, we are more likely to be more open and curious. We also tend to assume positive intent, stay in connection with the other person, resolve any disconnection—and move on. The alternative is to judge that person and be attached to being right about your judgment, which creates disconnection and moves you out of your OS.

One reframe technique I often use is called *magic words*. Magic words are key words or phrases that you decide on beforehand to help trigger an immediate perspective shift in a particular situation. For example, earlier I mentioned how Bill would use *savor* as a magic word to keep his attention focused during meetings.

On a personal level, I remember realizing that when I was distracted by work, I often got irritated if someone on my team needed to ask me a question. In those instances, it felt like an interruption of my day—I had so many things that I needed to get done. On top of that, I judged myself for being an asshole to the leader (or at least that's how my unfiltered inner critic talks). I did not want to feel that way, because I want to be a caring and helpful leader. I thought about what specific word would encapsulate how I wanted to feel and respond, and *mentor* immediately came to mind. Sharing my knowledge with my team is a way to mentor them, which is how I wanted to show up as a leader. Not irritated. Now, when I feel myself triggered, I say "mentor" in my head and my energy instantly shifts.

Reframing is a mental game I play every day. I have developed a heightened awareness of what thoughts are creating reactivity and stress. I take a step back and ask myself, *What word or phrase could be a more positive interpretation of this event?* I often see two parallel "movies" happening in my head. The first movie is me reacting out of habit and becoming reactive. The second movie is a new interpretation of the same event with minimal to no reactivity. Practicing this kind of reframing has had a huge impact on my happiness and well-being, and I've seen how it helps with clients as well.

Suggestions for using this tool

    a. Identify scenarios where you tend to be triggered and have not been able to change your automatic reaction.

    b. Imagine how you want to show up in that scenario.

    c. Think of a term or phrase that describes your ideal reaction. Be as specific as possible.

    d. Whenever you feel reactive in that scenario moving forward, repeat the word to yourself and allow it to shift your approach.

11. Whole-body yes

I discussed this tool briefly in chapter 9 when we looked at a mindset of authenticity. Katie and Gay Hendricks created a process of acting from a place of complete inner alignment as a "whole-body yes."[52]

We often do things out of fear, obligation, guilt, or judgment rather than doing what we really want. This is more like a partial-body yes, which is really a no. An incomplete yes can be tricky to catch because the reasoning we use to get ourselves there is usually reflective of deep-seated beliefs and ingrained behavior patterns.

Note that I am not encouraging you to live an exclusively emotion-driven or pleasure-driven life. I'm saying listen to your *head*, *heart*, and *gut* at the same time, and look for alignment. When you are making a decision about something, check in with all three. Resistance in any of these areas should result in a no. So many of my clients are "pleasers" who say yes to requests without really checking in with their head, heart, or gut. I ask them to mentally shift their default setting to saying no and to change that to a yes only after checking in with themselves to make sure there is no resistance.

If every ounce of your being is not saying "hell, yes" then you need to consider why you are feeling hesitancy. Consider what you might be doing out of fear, obligation, or guilt. Pay attention to your body when you think about things you have agreed to do. Is it constricted, tense, achy, or uncomfortable, or are you feeling spacious, light, and relaxed? Ask yourself who you said yes for—yourself or someone else?

Suggestions for using this tool

 a. For any decision, check for alignment between what your head thinks (logic), what your heart senses (feelings), and what your gut is telling you (intuition).

 b. If you don't have alignment, hold off on the decision. Evaluate the area of hesitancy. Do you need more information? Are you about to override a value? Is there a red flag your mind is trying not to see?

 c. Dig deep into why you are motivated to say yes when you really should say no. What does that urge tell you about your fears, needs, and insecurities? How would saying yes affect your aliveness?

 d. Make a decision based on all three centers of intelligence. You might need to say no entirely, or you might just need to tweak a few things before you get a whole-body yes. You won't know until you give equal weight to your entire self.

 e. Pay attention to your whole-body yes at work. Notice when you are saying yes when internally you have some resistance.

12. Journaling

This is a tool for self-reflection that invariably results in clarity and growth. There are many ways to journal. I don't tell my clients a specific way to do it or even a specific frequency. As I said regarding meditation, the best way to journal is the way that works for you.

Journaling helps us process our life experiences, especially the difficult ones. Research shows that expressing negative events through writing or verbal communication is far more beneficial than merely thinking about them. In her writings, researcher Sonja Lyubomirsky discusses how the act of putting our thoughts into words sparks a higher level of integration within ourselves, leads to a deeper understanding of the situation, allows us to form a cohesive narrative, and opens avenues for exploring potential solutions.

She also emphasizes that engaging in this kind of processing has a wide range of positive effects on our well-being. People who adopt writing or talking as a means of processing negative life experiences tend to experience more life satisfaction, better mental and physical health, and improved social functioning. On the other hand, those who just ruminate privately about these experiences often report a diminished sense of life satisfaction. She points out that by giving voice to our inner thoughts and emotions, we enable ourselves to find acceptance, resilience, and a path toward greater contentment and well-being.[53]

On a practical level, I encourage people to create a consistency that they can achieve 90 percent of the time. My house was littered with almost-blank journals because journaling daily was too much for me. I asked myself, *What commitment can I honor confidently?* The answer was once a week. I journal every Sunday, first thing in the morning. I look forward to it and rarely miss a week. I also review my calendar to see if there's anything worthy of adding. If there's something I want to write in my journal during the week, I make a quick note so that I'm sure to add it on Sunday. I find that journaling helps me reset for the week.

Suggestions for using this tool

  a. Decide where you want to write: a physical journal, your
     phone (such as a notes app), or your computer are good
     options.
  b. Decide a time and schedule. Whatever works for you is
     best, but it should be a time as free from distractions as
     possible. Remember, the goal is 90 percent consistency.
  c. Write whatever you want, but make sure you are brutally
     honest. For that reason, it's probably best to *not* plan on
     ever sharing the journal with anyone. I encourage you to
     include feelings, not just facts. Use the writing experience
     to draw more out of you than you might have admitted to
     yourself.
  d. Before you finish, check in with yourself. Did you get it all
     out, or is there still something inside that you need to put
     on paper?

13. Look back

I described this tool in chapter 11, when I shared about Paul's
tenacity in his aliveness journey. A look back is simply a reflection
on what another version of you would say about you today. You
can pick any time frame: you as a child, as a college student, as an
entrepreneur. You could even imagine a *future* version of yourself,
although technically that would be a look forward. What would
that version of you think of you today? How proud and impressed
would they feel? How encouraging would they be?

The value of the look back exercise is that my clients discover
that they have made more progress than they realized. It's another
way to self-distance. Almost without fail, their response is, "Better
than I could have imagined." That's important because the version
of you now may not have that assessment. The present-day you is
easily caught up in struggles, challenges, mistakes, and fears. You

are probably more focused on what you don't have, not what you
do have.

Suggestions for using this tool

    a. Imagine any version of yourself you'd like. I suggest ten
       years prior, at least. Think of how you were back then: your
       aspirations, your abilities, your experience.

    b. Imagine showing that version of yourself around your
       current life: your office, your income, your accomplish-
       ments, your influence. Imagine telling yourself about the
       challenges you've overcome and the risks you've taken.

    c. How does that version of you respond? Can you feel the
       emotion that person feels toward you? Imagine their admi-
       ration and their gratitude.

    d. Finally, allow yourself to feel those things toward the
       present-day version of you.

14. Wall of Gratitude

This is a practical tool to keep you in the right frame of mind. Find
a wall that you will see daily, and fill it with photos of you feeling
alive, of reminders of what you love about life, and of things you've
accomplished.

This doesn't have to be a physical wall. You can also keep a
document or file with quotes from people who have thanked you
for your work or spoken highly of you.

The point here is not narcissism. It's counteracting the inner
critic. When you are discouraged, the critic comes out in full force.
Having objective reminders of your success, impact, and talent
can be invaluable in those moments.

Gratitude is a powerful tool for aliveness because it almost
instantly shifts your energy and focus. Negativity is no match for
thankfulness. And no matter how bad things are going, you can

always find something to be grateful for. I'm not saying that makes the pain or fear go away, but it gives you perspective, and often that's all you need.

Suggestions for using this tool
a. As described above, pick a wall (or filing system) for your display.
b. Get started by putting pictures and/or quotes up that will encourage you.
c. Over time, add to your wall.
d. When you feel discouraged or you're dealing with self-doubt, return to your wall. Don't just look or read: feel the original emotions you felt when you experienced those things for the first time. Every time I look at my Wall of Gratitude, I slow down. I smile. My heart opens. I feel joy. I feel love. What pictures can you find to evoke similar emotions and experiences?

15. Kindness and connection

This is a simple tool, but it's one of my favorites, so I'll end with this one. Being nice to people is a powerful tool for your aliveness. We discussed this in chapter 12, when we discussed a mindset of love.

If you are in reactivity, often all it takes to get out of that state is a kind word or gesture toward someone else. It might not get you all the way back to your OS, but it's a step in the right direction, and it's entirely under your control.

The very act of considering other people gets you out of your own head. It's that simple. It shifts your focus from what you can't do to what you can do; from what you don't have to what you do have. It sparks gratitude and joy. It gives you purpose and value. It improves your opinion of yourself. It increases connection with other people, which is a basic human need.

I could go on and on about the power of kindness and human connection. When my clients are sharing a story about a situation that is causing them stress or reactivity, I'll ask them, "Is your heart open or closed? What can you think of that will help open your heart?" I like to ask my clients to see the world through the other person's eyes. It also helps to try to understand that the other person was doing their best, they might have had a hard day, or they are focused on something different. It's always valuable to see situations from the perspective of other people.

Suggestions for using this tool

a. When you feel reactive, or if you have left your OS and are feeling lost in self-doubt, discouragement, or any other negative feeling, remind yourself that the world does not revolve around you, and you have a lot to be grateful for.

b. Make a small list of things you could do now to add value to someone else or improve their quality of life. These things should be something immediately doable and within your means. Don't add more stress and guilt to your plate by trying to do things that are too ambitious or long-term.

c. Pick one thing from your list and do it as soon as possible.

d. Pay attention to the effect you had on that person's day. Remind yourself that you are good, you have power, and you are making a difference.

That's a whirlwind tour through a very full toolbox. There are some practical ideas about maintaining and expanding your aliveness. These are strategies and approaches that have produced visible results with the hundreds of CEOs and business leaders I've worked with, and I use them all in my own life as well. They are relatively easy to use and usually bring quick, tangible results.

As I said before, *the best tools are the ones you use.* Please experiment with these strategies and see what works for you. The tools are not the point—you are. So use the tools if they help you, but don't lock yourself into methods or steps.

There are many other strategies for self-awareness and self-fulfillment that could also be useful for your aliveness journey. Multiple fields of study—including psychology, medicine, religion, sociology, and more—have made contributions to living happy, healthy, whole lives, and I encourage you to continue learning how to facilitate your aliveness from a range of sources.

Above all, you should know as much as possible about *you.* You're the most qualified to know yourself, listen to yourself, and lead yourself. While tools like these help, and while coaches and therapists and other experts can come alongside you as needed, ultimately this is your life and your aliveness.

Would you have it any other way?

THE FUTURE IS ALIVE

"Living All In" isn't about experiencing immediate, blissful success in everything you do. It's about focusing on your day-to-day experience. It's about the little things you do to create more aliveness in your relationships and interactions. Living All In is about focusing on how you can bring a better version of yourself into everything you do, every day.

. . . .

What I've realized is the importance of taking these tools (Anchoring Mindsets, Optimal State, accelerants, Wall of Gratitude, etc.) and making them a *daily practice*. If we aren't practicing our mindset every day, we naturally fall back to our patterns of reactivity rather than feeling alive.

. . . .

People will notice the difference. Your team, your significant other, your parents or kids, your friends, your clients—they are watching, and they will notice and appreciate how you show up in the world differently. I believe your aliveness will have a positive impact on them because they need you to be at your best, and they'll be inspired by your honesty and courage to become better versions of themselves.

Do you remember Jill, the hardworking leader with a strained relationship with her father? She recently reached out to let me know how differently she relates to her father and her children now, compared to where she was several years ago. She has been making a conscious effort to be fully present and engaged when she is at home. She shared with me that her family followed my custom for birthdays recently, and everyone at the table appreciated her. All of her children and husband affirmed her, and tears filled her eyes. She told me she had always dreamed of being seen and appreciated in just those ways, and their words were proof she had accomplished that.

That is Living All In. That is being fully alive.

Remember, life is by nature unpredictable and filled with risk. So it's natural that we want to feel in control, even over things and people that we can't control. Think of how much of your reactivity is based on how others act and think, wanting them to be different. Yet that is completely out of your hands.

Aliveness is in your control.

That's what I want you to take away from this book. Aliveness is *always* within you. If your current business succeeds or fails, you can still be alive. If you pursue a dream and that succeeds or fails, you can still be alive. If life throws you curveballs, or if you throw life curveballs, you can still be alive.

. . . .

Aliveness is in your control.

. . . .

I can't speak to the future of your career, but I know that the future of the inner you is capable of being fully and vibrantly alive. Commit to living all in, no matter where that takes you.

See beyond the expectations and obligations that try to define you, push back on those things, and fight to be the most authentic version of yourself.

Dig deep inside yourself until you find your unique aliveness, and then you treasure and nurture and explore and expand that feeling until it becomes the filter that guides your life.

Bring the best version of yourself into your day-to-day experience by aligning your mindsets and actions with the things that make you most alive.

Aliveness is always there, deep inside you.

It's up to you to choose it.

I want to end with one of my all-time favorite quotes. When I'm having a really tough day, when I'm reactive and can't seem to find my way back to my OS, I remind myself of this phrase that I heard Lin Brehmer, a well-loved DJ at Chicago classic rock station WXRT for over three decades, repeat many times over the years.

Take nothing for granted. It's great to be alive.

GLOSSARY

Accelerants: small, practical actions that help you activate, sustain, extend, and maximize your aliveness. They connect you to yourself in a way that brings clarity to your mind and energy to your body. They activate alignment between the *doing* part of you and the *being* part of you.

Aliveness: a state of being characterized by bringing the best version of yourself into your day-to-day experience through identifying and adopting mindsets and actions that align with your special way of being fully alive.

Aliveness Mindset: an internal conviction that aliveness is desirable and possible, as well as the commitment to pursue and develop aliveness in your life. This overarching mindset is the outer ring in the Circle of Aliveness, and it consists of seven elements: ownership, openness, awareness, authenticity, courage, tenacity, and love.

Aliveness Practice: the middle ring of the Circle of Aliveness. It refers to the practical work of pursuing aliveness, starting with defining what it means to you and then learning how you experience it most fully. It includes your Anchoring Mindsets.

Anchoring Mindsets (AMs): the particular mental models, values, or drivers that underlie your aliveness. These mindsets are specific to you: they are essential components of your value system and your inner motivations that help move you toward aliveness, regardless of how difficult of a challenge you might be facing.

Circle of Aliveness: a diagram or model that illustrates the relationship between an Aliveness Mindset (how you think and feel), an Aliveness Practice (what you do), and your Optimal State (what you experience as a result).

LAI Tools: a collection of strategies that help you return to, remain in, or expand your Optimal State. See chapter 18 for a detailed explanation and list.

Mindset: how your brain develops and maintains your unique perspective. It is the beliefs and attitudes that shape the lens you see the world through and that guide your behavior, choose your priorities, direct your decisions, and lead you to set and pursue your goals.

Optimal State (OS): the center of the Circle of Aliveness. Your OS is your distinctive brand or flavor of aliveness. It refers to how, when, and why you feel most alive. It is you at your best. It's the version of you that is aligned inside and out, that experiences life fully and brings its entire self to everything.

Reactivity: an automatic, triggered response to a perceived threat. Reactivity occurs when we have a spontaneous response to what is occurring in and around us.

ACKNOWLEDGMENTS

MAKING THE CAREER CHANGE TO BECOMING AN EXECUTIVE COACH would not have been possible without the support of so many. I am forever grateful for those who encouraged me all along the way and those who hired me to work with their leaders within their companies.

To my wife, Judy; our three daughters, Hallie, Rachel, Shana; and our "son/dog," Riley, for their love all along the way. You cheered me on when I needed it most. You believed in me before I really believed it. To my mom, Shirley; brother, Barry; and sister, Carrie, who always supported my personal growth.

To Grace Clayton, who offhandedly said, "You should write a book" after I guided her through the Living All In exercise. Once she said that, my body lit up. Almost three years later, the book "Aliveness Mindset" is a reality.

Special thanks to Jim Dethmer, Diana Chapman, and Erica Schreiber of the Conscious Leadership Group, and all of the coaches on the team. I learned so much from each of you about how to be a world-class coach and a more compassionate human being. I am grateful for having the opportunity to work with so many talented leaders on behalf of CLG. Most importantly, thank you for reminding me what it feels like to play and feel alive.

To all of my friends that are a part of the conscious community.

To my YPO forum members, both current (Jenni Suvari, Britt Whitfield, Mike Shedivy, Joey Lansing, Joe Gaffigan, Kerryann Minton, Jamie Henry) and past when I made the career change (Eric

Langshur, Andrew Swinand, Mike Elrad, John Benevides). Your feedback and emotional support was instrumental to my success.

Special thanks to Eric Langshur. Thank you for your friendship, insight, generosity, and guidance. You are the ultimate illuminator.

To Dr. Lyle Berkowitz, my first client.

To my long-time clients: RMB Capital, Dick Burridge, Jennifer Rydwelski, Jeannette Gawrisch, Dr. Rahul Khare, Kelly O'Connell, Nick Saccaro, and Matt Bluhm.

To Nathan Olivas, Joe Almon, Randy Grote, Matt Perry, Marc Brenner, David Brenner, and Todd Buterbaugh. Thank you for believing in me.

To my high school and college friends whose friendship spanning several decades still means everything to me.

To Kathie Mills, my executive assistant (and more) who has supported me since the beginning of my coaching practice. You have made my life easier and have allowed me to focus on building my business and providing radical support to all of my clients.

To all of those who graciously agreed to read advance copies of the book and gave me incredible feedback to elevate the book to a level I'm proud of (Alison Lee, Valerie Atkin, Eric Langshur, Jillia Wharton, Katie Clune, and Laura Kunberger).

To all of the leaders in the Aliveness Circle Forum who have been with me since the beginning, Alissa Cardone, Katie Clune, Melissa Diglio, Laura Kunberger, and Lisa Sobilo. Thank you for all of your trust, love, and support.

To Michelle Thompson, who was invaluable in helping with early drafts of this book.

Thank you to Whitney Gossett and Clint Greeleaf at Content Capital who helped me navigate the publishing world.

To my brothers and coleaders of The Men's Way, Tim Day, Gentzy Franz, Marc Malnati, Kim Redding, and Jim Placio.

I also want to thank the many thought leaders who have inspired me and whose work I have integrated as part of the Aliveness Mindset process. I honor your work by including your ideas in Aliveness Mindset as well as in my coaching sessions and during my company talks.

Thank you to Jonathan Merkh, Jennifer Gingerich, Phil Newman, and Landon Dickerson at Forefront Books to push this project forward into what it is today. Thanks also to the team at Simon and Schuster for getting this book into the hands of readers!

ABOUT THE AUTHOR

JACK CRAVEN HAS ALWAYS SHAPED HIS PROFESSIONAL JOURNEY around his passions. Starting out as a trial lawyer with the Chicago State's Attorney Office, he moved into private practice and later took on the role of CEO for his family's business for nearly two decades. Yet his move into executive coaching stands out as the most challenging—and rewarding—chapter of his career. It was during this time that Jack created his "Living All In" philosophy. He has utilized his extensive professional and personal growth journey to empower individuals to discover deeper purpose, joy, and happiness in their lives.

Since 2007, Jack has also been an active member and Certified Facilitator for the Young Presidents' Organization (YPO), the world's leading community for chief executives.

Just as passionate about his personal pursuits, Jack loves keeping fit, reading, volunteering in his Chicago community, and spending quality time with his wife, three daughters, and Riley! This is his debut book.

NOTES

1   Some names and details have been changed, but the situations described are very real.

2   If you're familiar with Ross Geller's angst in the couch-moving scene of the sitcom *Friends*, you get this exclamatory use of "Pivot!" right away.

3   Robert Waldinger and Marc Schulz, *The Good Life: Lessons from the World's Longest Study on Happiness* (London: Ebury Publishing, 2023), 15.

4   Waldinger and Schulz, 124.

5   Carol S. Dweck, *Mindset: The New Psychology of Success* (New York: Random House, 2006).

6   David Robson, *The Expectation Effect: How Your Mindset Can Change Your World* (New York: Henry Holt, 2022), 31.

7   Robson, 7.

8   James Clear, "3-2-1: Eliminating Tasks, Optimizing for Your Interests, and Sharing Knowledge," James Clear (blog), July 28, 2022, https://jamesclear.com/3-2-1/july-28-2022.

9   John H. Flavell, "Metacognition and Cognitive Monitoring: A New Area of Cognitive-Developmental Inquiry," *American Psychologist* 34, no. 10 (October 1, 1979): 906–11.

10 Diana Chapman, Jim Dethmer, and Kaley Klemp, *The 15 Commitments of Conscious Leadership: A New Paradigm for Sustainable Success* (n.p.: Conscious Leadership Group/Kaley Warner Klemp, 2015).

11 Julian B. Rotter, "Generalized Expectancies for Internal versus External Control of Reinforcement," *Psychological Monographs: General and Applied* 80, no. 1 (January 1, 1966): 1–28, https://doi.org/10.1037/h0092976.

12 Benjamin M. Galvin, Amy E. Randel, Brian J. Collins, and Russell E. Johnson, "Changing the Focus of Locus (of Control): A Targeted Review of the Locus of Control Literature and Agenda for Future Research," *Journal of Organizational Behavior* 39, no. 7 (September 1, 2018): 820–33, https://doi.org/10.1002/job.2275.

13 P. Bregman and H. Jacobson, "Feedback Isn't Enough to Help Your Employees Grow," *Harvard Business Review*, December 10, 2021: 1–7.

14 Sindu Padmanabhan, "The Impact of Locus of Control on Workplace Stress and Job Satisfaction: A Pilot Study on Private-Sector Employees," *Current Research in Behavioral Sciences* 2 (November 1, 2021): 100026, https://doi.org/10.1016/j.crbeha.2021.100026.

15 Investment Weekly News, "New Emerging Markets Findings from Science University of Malaysia Outlined (Effect of Open-Mindedness and Humble Behavior on Innovation: Mediator Role of Learning)," November 13, 2021, Gale OneFile: Business.

16 Julia Galef, *The Scout Mindset: Why Some People See Things Clearly and Others Don't* (New York: Little, Brown, 2021).

17 Joseph LeDoux, *Anxious: The Modern Mind in the Age of Anxiety* (New York: Simon & Schuster, 2015).

18 Michael A. Singer, *The Untethered Soul: The Journey beyond Yourself* (Oakland, CA: New Harbinger, 2007), 62.

19 Singer, 72.

20 Hale Dwoskin and Lester Levenson, *The Sedona Method: Your Key to Lasting Happiness, Success, Peace and Emotional WellBeing* (n.p.: SCB Distributors, 2020).

21 Jim Dethmer, "Review of Commit to Sourcing Approval, Control, and Security from Within," The Conscious Leadership Group 2019, https://conscious.is/video/commit-to-sourcing-approval-control-and-security-from-within.

22 Brené Brown, *The Gifts of Imperfection: 10th Anniversary Edition* (Center City, MN: Hazelden, 2022), 66.

23 E. Tory Higgins, "Self-Discrepancy: A Theory Relating Self and Affect," *Psychological Review* 94, no. 3 (1987): 319.

24 Daniel H. Pink, *The Power of Regret: How Looking Backward Moves Us Forward* (New York: Penguin Random House, 2022), 173.

25 Victoria Labalme, *Risk Forward: Embrace the Unknown and Unlock Your Hidden Genius* (Carlsbad, CA: Hay House, 2021), 8.

26 Quoted by Stephen R. Covey; see his account at https://www.viktorfrankl.org/assets/pdf/Covey_Intro_to_Pattakos_Prisoners.pdf.

27 Brené Brown, *Daring Greatly* (New York: Penguin: Avery, 2012).

28 Ethan Kross, *Chatter: The Voice in Our Head, Why It Matters, and How to Harness It* (New York: Crown, 2021).

29 Angela Duckworth, *Grit: The Power of Passion and Perseverance* (New York: Scribner, 2016).

30 Arghavan Salles, Geoffrey L. Cohen, and Claudia M. Mueller, "The Relationship Between Grit and Resident Well-Being," *The American Journal of Surgery* 207, no. 2 (2014): 251–54.

31 Theodore Roosevelt, "Citizenship in a Republic" (aka "The Man in the Arena"), speech at the Sorbonne, Paris, France, April 23, 1910, https://www.theodorerooseveltcenter.org/Learn-About-TR/TR-Encyclopedia/Culture-and-Society/Man-in-the-Arena.aspx.

32 Bell Hooks, *All about Love: New Visions,* Bell Hooks Love Trilogy (New York: HarperCollins, 2001), 36.

33 Waldinger and Schulz, *The Good Life: Lessons from the World's Longest Scientific Study of Happiness,* 29.

34 Jennifer G. Berger and Carolyn Coughlin, *Unleash Your Complexity Genius: Growing Your Inner Capacity to Lead* (Stanford, CA: Stanford University Press, 2022).

35 Kelly-Ann Allen, Margaret L. Kern, Christopher S. Rozek, Dennis M. McInerney, and George M. Slavich, "Belonging: A Review of Conceptual Issues, an Integrative Framework, and Directions for Future Research," *Australian Journal of Psychology* 73, no. 1 (January 2, 2021): 87–102, https://doi.org/10.1080/00049530.2021.1883409.

36 Leigh L. Thompson, *Making the Team: A Guide for Managers,* 6th ed. (New York: Pearson, 2018).

37 Robson, *Expectation Effect,* 31.

38 Mihaly Csikszentmihalyi, *Flow: The Psychology of Optimal Experience* (United Kingdom: HarperCollins, 2008).

39 Jeanne Nakamura, Dwight C. K. Tse, and Shannon Shankland, "Flow: The Experience of Intrinsic Motivation," *The Oxford Handbook of Human Motivation,* 2nd ed. (New York: Oxford University Press, 2019), 169–85.

40 Eric Langshur and Nate Klemp, *Start Here: Master the Lifelong Habit of Wellbeing,* Kindle Edition (New York: Gallery, 2016).

41 Susan Bulzoni, "Breathing Exercises: Three to Try: 4-7-8 Breath: Andrew Weil, M.D.," DrWeil.com, February 22, 2022, https://www.drweil.com/health-wellness/body-mind-spirit/stress-anxiety/breathing-three-exercises.

42 Kristin D. Neff, "Self-Compassion: Theory, Method, Research, and Intervention," *Annual Review of Psychology* 74 (2023): 194.

43 Neff, 193–218.

44 Pink, *Power of Regret.*

45 Jia Wei Zhang and Serena Chen, "Self-Compassion Promotes Personal Improvement From Regret Experiences Via Acceptance," *Personality and Social Psychology Bulletin* 42, no. 2 (2016): 244–58.

46 Kristin D. Neff, Stephanie S. Rude, and Kristin L. Kirkpatrick, "An Examination of Self-Compassion in Relation to Positive Psychological Functioning and Personality Traits," *Journal of Research in Personality* 41, no. 4 (2007): 908–16.

47 Kristin D. Neff, "Self-Compassion, Self-Esteem, and Well-Being," *Social and Personality Psychology Compass* 5, no. 1 (2011): 1–12.

48 Pink, *Power of Regret,* 178.

49 Timothy Ferriss, *Tribe of Mentors: Short Life Advice from the Best in the World* (United Kingdom: Ebury Publishing, 2017), 561.

50 James Clear, "3-2-1: Outsmarting Yourself, Staying Adaptable, and Choosing More Empowering Self-Talk," James Clear (blog), October 20, 2022, https://jamesclear.com/3-2-1/october-20-2022.

51 As quoted by his son, Steven M.R. Covey, and Rebecca R. Merrill, *The SPEED of Trust: The One Thing That Changes Everything* (United Kingdom: Free Press, 2008), 13.

52 Katie and Gay Hendricks, The Hendricks Institute, https://hendricks.com/.

53 Sonia Lyubomirsky, Lorie Sousa, and Rene Dickerhoof, "The Costs and Benefits of Writing, Talking, and Thinking About Life's Triumphs and Defeats," *Journal of Personality and Social Psychology* 90, no. 4 (2006): 692.